# little walks
# BIG ADVENTURES

## 50+ Ideas for
## Exploring with Toddlers

---

### ERIN BUHR, MEd

Copyright ©2018 Erin Buhr

Published by Gryphon House, Inc.
P. O. Box 10, Lewisville, NC 27023
800.638.0928; fax 877.638.7576
WWW.GRYPHONHOUSE.COM

Gryphon House books are available for special premiums and sales promotions as well as for fund-raising use. Special editions or book excerpts also can be created to specifications. For details, call 800.638.0928.

Gryphon House, Inc., cannot be held responsible for damage, mishap, or injury incurred during the use of or because of activities in this book. Appropriate and reasonable caution and adult supervision of children involved in activities and corresponding to the age and capability of each child involved are recommended at all times. Do not leave children unattended at any time. Observe safety and caution at all times.

Library of Congress Cataloging-in-Publication Data
Names: Buhr, Erin, author.
Title: Little walks, big adventures : 50+ ideas for exploring with toddlers /
   by Erin Buhr, M.Ed.
Description: Lewinsville, NC : Gryphon House, Inc., 2018. | Includes
   bibliographical references.
Identifiers: LCCN 2017037290 | ISBN 9780876597576 (pbk.)
Subjects: LCSH: Early childhood education--Activity programs. |
   Toddlers--Development.
Classification: LCC LB1139.35.A37 B84 2018 | DDC 372.13--dc23 LC record available at https://lccn.loc.gov/2017037290

FOR
N, J, & A
MY BEST ADVENTURE

# Contents

## Home and Community

## Vehicles

# Our World

# Animals

# Introduction

When we are born the whole world is new. Infants and toddlers are learning every moment. They are soaking in the world around them: the sights, sounds, smells, interactions, languages, and textures. Everything is new. Everything is interesting. For this reason, everything is also curriculum.

When working with or parenting toddlers, it is not just colors and shapes that we are teaching them, but it is also how to interact with others, how to wash their hands, and how to put on their shoes. These are all-important developmental skills.

I think the world is a magical place. Sure there is trash, poverty, traffic, and meanness in the world, but if you look for it, there is beauty that can far overshadow the ugly. I want my children to see that world. I want them to have experiences. I want them to understand that they are a small beautiful part in a much larger world. I want them to learn from real things in the real world.

It has long been taught that young children learn best through hands-on experiences. As educational reformer John Dewey so plainly explained, "Experience is education." Often this is translated to using one's hands to learn in a classroom. This is a valid approach, but I believe taking children out into the world is often the purest hands-on experience.

As toddlers, my twins adored trucks, trains, cars, buses, or anything that moved. Most toddlers do. We read endless books from the library about trains and trucks, blew on pretend train whistles, drove play cars around our play space, and sang "The Wheels on the Bus" constantly, but these are not the experiences they talk about.

My son spent more than two months remembering our trip on a bus when he was a toddler. Watching real trucks dig up a construction site maintained their toddler attention for an hour. Hearing a real flamingo shout at the zoo was better than Eric Carle's fluting illustrations. As Holly Hughes, author of *Frommer's 500 Places to Take Your Kids Before They Grow Up*, points out, "Awakening that sense of wonder is what travel is all about, for adults as well as children." Seeing that these cool things exist in real life is what makes them intriguing for children. The world fascinates them, motivates them, and inspires them.

Furthermore, providing the greatest range of experiences for a topic has been found to be beneficial for young learners. These adventures are so rich with language and sights and sounds they can cause natural explosions in language, reasoning, and other areas of development if you are willing to engage with the toddler as you go.

Researcher Patricia Bauer studies children's learning and memory. Her findings, as described by author and educator Ellen Galinsky, suggest that "one of the things that we've found that helps babies to remember is being allowed to be engaged in the activity." When they see something more than once and are experiencing something that is meaningful and purposeful, they remember it.

From this, I find myself inspired to explore with my toddlers. To see the world through a toddler's eyes is to see its beauty, wonder, and possibility all over again.

# How to Use This Book

The book is divided into four main adventure topics: Home and Community, Vehicles, Animals, and Our World. Within each theme there are thirteen adventures, each with corresponding activities. This book is intended to give you ideas for following common toddler interests.

The adventures are intended for toddlers roughly aged fifteen to thirty-six months of age of all developmental abilities. Throughout the book there are tips to make these adventures and ideas accessible for the different abilities and special needs of children in this age group.

There are ideas for every week of the year, but do not feel as if you need to follow the order in this book. It is intended as inspiration for trips and activities that you can do with toddlers. Try different things, but also do the ones you love over and over again. Toddlers thrive on repetition. Children can take in only so much in one trip. They will notice something different every time they go to the same zoo or neighborhood spot.

To get started, pick an adventure that sounds interesting or fits the current interests of your toddler(s). If a child is interested in helping you cook, consider a trip to the bakery. If a child loves animals, start with the pet-store trip.

After each adventure, there are several related activity ideas. These can also be done in any order, but they may give you some ideas of how to extend children's learning at home or in the classroom. These are primarily open-ended activities. They address the different developmental areas including physical, social/emotional, cognitive, language, and self-help. These activities encourage you to follow your toddlers' lead and enjoy the process of learning what they find important at this time, rather than directing them toward a specific set of knowledge or any sort of product. The idea is to help them process and think more deeply about the experiences they have had on your adventures.

Many of the activities can be done with most of the adventures, if slightly adapted. These activities have all been done with groups of toddlers aged fifteen to thirty-six months. I have worked with various groups in different settings and understand that some groups or settings are more challenging to have routine adventures, but it is possible to some extent in every location where I have worked.

My biggest tip is to creatively find ways to reduce group sizes wherever possible. While working in a corporate child care center, my co teachers and I worked hard to schedule opportunities for teachers to work in smaller groups of seven children instead of our whole group of twenty-one toddlers by being creative with outside time and sharing other classrooms. The smaller groups were quieter and easier for many of the activities described in this book. While it is possible to march fifteen toddlers through a college campus to a city farmers market, that would have been infinitely easier with only five. In another setting I was incredibly fortunate to have ratios as low as 1:4 for younger toddlers, and while I truly believe this is the ideal, I understand and have more experience working with the opposite end of this spectrum. Be flexible in challenging your current schedule, spaces, and procedures. I promise the rewards of smaller groups are worth it.

Your center and director will have limitations, your setting might not have all of the adventure ideas nearby, and your resources will likely be limited. Your goal is to do your best to think creatively to offer your toddlers more hands-on, real experiences, however you can do that best.

Rather than seeing an idea and thinking it is impossible, let it help you think about what is possible. Let this book inspire you to take your toddlers' interests and experiences and blend them into hands-on, child-led, creative learning.

## BUT What if...

**My toddler likes to eat bugs**
Redirect the little one who is interested in putting everything he sees into his mouth.

**The children get cranky on a walk**
Pack a small activity book or a lovey in case a child needs something else to occupy her.

Make sure children are fed and changed before you begin your walk, but always travel with a diaper bag. Don't travel too far with toddlers (they can typically handle about a mile) to avoid tantrums on your trip.

**A toddler gets a boo-boo**
I recommend packing a small first-aid kit in your diaper bag for those minor injuries.

For more ideas on how to handle similar situations with toddlers, be sure to read the "Consider" section of each adventure.

**Home, family, community**

These are the first experiences a young child has. As toddlers work to figure out who they are and what their role is in the world, they observe and imitate the people around them. You will often see toddlers swaddling baby dolls, pretending to talk on the phone, or cooking imaginary dishes.

# Home and Community

# Neighborhood Walk

**W**hether the neighborhood is new to you or not, it is less known to the toddlers. Go for a walk. Don't have an agenda or any place to be. Just walk and see what interests your toddlers. The first time I did this with our fifteen-month-olds, they were interested in the colored covers for the gas pipes on the sidewalk, so we found more and talked about colors. On another walk they were fascinated by acorns and pinecones, so we collected a bunch and brought them home.

As you prepare to go on your walk, talk with the children about where you are going. Mention things you might see along the way.

**BRING**

Bring along wipes, bags for collecting items that interest the children, paper and pencil to write down the children's questions and observations, and a camera to record your adventure.

**CONSIDER**

If your surrounding area is unsafe for walking, consider pushing a large stroller to a location better suited for toddler exploration and then letting little ones jump out to walk and explore.

For children who have difficulty walking, include them by bringing a paraprofessional or teacher's aide to push their wheelchairs or pull them in a wagon as other children walk.

**NOTICE**

When you head out the door, comment on the weather, sounds you hear, and anything else that captures your or the children's attention.

As you walk, pay close attention to what the children are looking at or listening to. Come alongside them and explore with them.

Pay attention to time and distance. Don't wander too far and then have to struggle home with tired, crabby children.

# Activities

## Make a BOOK about Your WALK

Making a book of your trip anywhere is an easy and fun way to continue talking about your adventures long after they are through. I am including it here because this activity would work for every adventure included in this book.

### Materials

| | |
|---|---|
| Camera | Printer |
| Paper | Marker |
| Tape | Glue stick |

3-hole punch and rings or
   yarn and ribbon
Index cards or card stock
Clear contact paper (optional)
Scissors (adult use)

### What to Do

1. Take photos of your walk—especially the parts that interest your toddlers.

2. Print the photos.

3. Make a book by gluing the photos to index cards or to card stock.

4. Label each page using a marker.

5. For durability, cover each page of the book with clear contact paper.

6. Use a hole punch and rings or yarn or ribbon to bind the pages into a book.

7. Look through the book as often as you like to remind your toddlers about the adventure. This repetition will help further their vocabulary learning when you discuss what you saw together in the neighborhood.

## CHALK and TRUCK Neighborhood

This is a simple outside activity that brings a toy you would normally use inside to a different space to encourage new play.

### Materials

Chalk
Toy trucks or cars

### What to Do

1. Draw roads on the ground outside, and set out trucks and cars.

2. Talk about driving around your neighborhood, and model stopping at stop signs as you play.

3. Consider looking through your walk book together to see what else you could add to your neighborhood. (Painter's tape on the floor works too, if you want to do this inside.)

# Grocery Store

Children are often carted along when their caregivers go to the grocery store every week. Whether you find ways to include them in your weekly trip—for example, give them their own list, have them help count fruit as you put it in a bag, and let them make choices—or make a special trip to the store for the ingredients for one recipe, the grocery store is a great adventure destination.

**BRING**  For younger children, give them a visual list with pictures along with words.

**CONSIDER**  Have set, firm rules for the store. Can they walk with you? Do they need to hold your hand? Do they have to ride in the stroller or cart? Don't give them a choice where there isn't one, and they will learn not to fight you.

**NOTICE**  There is so much to learn at the store (vocabulary, currency, counting). The self-help skills and knowledge-building opportunities abound. I highly recommend, at least once, going through the entire process from start to finish with your toddler or class. Pick a recipe, make a list of ingredients you need, gather them at the store together, and take everything back and cook together.

# Activities

Imaginary play is a developmentally important way that children practice and cement new ideas.

## GROCERY Store Dramatic PLAY

### What to Do

1. Take the pretend play food that you use in your play kitchen and lay it out on shelves.

2. Add bags or baskets for shoppers and ones for bagging groceries.

3. Put play money or green paper labeled as money in the area.

4. Model for your toddlers the different roles of shopping.

### Materials

Recycled kitchen materials such as empty cereal boxes, spice jars, etc. Save yours or ask parents for donations.
Paper or cloth grocery bags
Play money or green construction paper
Toy cash registers

---

Counting and other math skills are easily integrated into cooking activities.

## Counting FRUIT

### What to Do

1. Encourage your toddlers to help you count a certain number of berries while you make a fruit salad. Counting is an early math skill that engages toddlers' cognition.

2. Count out one apple for each person for lunch or two crackers for each toddler at snack time.

### Materials

Simple foods such as fruit or vegetables

# Restaurant

think all parents have a love/hate relationship with taking young children out to eat. On one hand, toddlers love it. They love watching the people. They love ordering their food. They love drinks with straws.

On the other hand, their behavior leaves something to be desired. They are often too busy watching people to eat their food. They usually spill those drinks with straws. They have a hard time sitting still long enough to wait for their food.

That being said, restaurants are a part of their world and often a part of life. There are also a lot of things to learn at a restaurant, including how to order a meal and how to entertain yourself while you wait.

**BRING** Pack things to do while they wait for food, such as magnetic dress-up dolls, Wikki Stix, and stickers.

**CONSIDER**
- If you are doing this with a class, make sure you go when the restaurant is not busy. Midmorning is best.
- Scope out the place in advance to make sure there is enough table space available for your whole group.
- Make sure the restaurant is accessible if you have any children in wheelchairs.
- Look at the menu to determine what you could order with a limited budget, and keep any allergies or dietary restrictions in mind. Perhaps the children could order a juice or order something that is sharable that they could eat as a snack.

**NOTICE** One of the ways to make visiting a restaurant easier with children is to include them. It is so tempting to do everything for them. Don't. Instead, read the menu together. Encourage them to order. Some servers have more patience for this than others, but starting around age three my children began ordering for themselves. While you wait for the server, coach them on what to say so their words are ready.

# Activities

## DIY Menu Play PROP

This is another example of using pretend play to practice new skills learned on an adventure. It is an opportunity to practice the vocabulary and routines involved in ordering food.

### Materials
Card stock or cardboard
Magazines or ads with
    pictures of foods
Glue sticks
Markers

### What to Do

1. Tear out pages of ads or magazine pages so they are easier to cut or tear. With younger toddlers, involve them in picking the foods and helping you tear them out to engage them in a self-help activity. With older toddlers, have them choose and tear out the foods themselves.

2. Have your child help you make menus by picking out the food and gluing it down to the paper.

3. Use the marker to label the food item and add a price to your menu.

4. Then place the menus in your pretend play area. You will want to have at least one menu per two to three toddlers who play in the area at a time.

## GLUE Plate ART

Since your toddlers did all that great work tearing out pictures of food, use the leftover photos for some simple crafting.

### What to Do

### Materials
1 paper plate per child
Pictures of food
1 glue stick per child

1. Make a pretend meal by choosing, cutting (or tearing), and gluing pictures of food to your plate.

2. Gluing is a skill. Regardless of what kind of glue you use, toddlers will need patient instruction that will not be magically learned in just one exposure to the material. Remind them calmly and patiently to use just a little dab on each piece. You will need to repeat this again and again at first.

This is an open-ended art activity that allows children to create a lovely addition to your home or classroom.

# PRINTMAKING
## Tablecloth

## What to Do

1. Cut the sponges into shapes ahead of time.

2. Take a large piece of cloth and lay it out on a tabletop or on the floor.

3. Let the children use the sponges cut into shapes and acrylic paint to decorate the cloth.

4. Let it dry overnight and then it should be ready to use.

### Materials
Large piece of cloth
Sponges
Scissors (adult use only)
Acrylic paint

# ———— Home and Community Booklist ————

From *The Sounds Around Town* to *Knuffle Bunny*, these titles will help you and your toddlers further explore the themes of home and community. I recommend reading them as you work your way through the adventures to help you and your little ones think about where you live and what goes on in your world.

*Big Jimmy's Kum Kau Chinese Take Out* by Ted Lewin

*Clothesline Clues to Jobs People Do* by Kathryn Heling and Deborah Hembrook

*An Evening at Alfie's* by Shirley Hughes

*Everywhere Babies* by Susan Meyers

*How Did That Get in My Lunchbox? The Story of Food* by Chris Butterworth

*Julius: The Baby of the World* by Kevin Henkes

*Knuffle Bunny: A Cautionary Tale* by Mo Willems

*Otto the Book Bear* by Katie Cleminson

*Phoebe and Digger* by Tricia Springstubb

*The Shape of Things* by Dayle Ann Dodds

*The Sounds Around Town* by Maria Carluccio

*Ten Little Fingers and Ten Little Toes* by Mem Fox

# Farmers' Market

**F**armers' markets are fun places to try different foods, explore currency, and learn about making transactions. They are also colorful, filled with different people, and alive with sounds. Many of the things you would learn about at a farmers' market are similar to those at a grocery store. The process is similar, but you get to talk to the actual farmers. You get to make more purchases. You often have more choices. You usually get to shop in the open air.

**BRING** Make a list of a few things you want to get at the farmers' market that you can look for together. A list (visual for younger toddlers) will help you focus.

Bring a range of bills for easy purchasing. Plan to purchase various fruits for the "Color-Themed Snack" and the "New Fruit Exploration" activities.

**CONSIDER** Before you go on the field trip, and again before you enter the market, outline specific expectations. In our case, we walked fifteen toddlers to the farmers' market with three staff members. Each group of five held on to a rope as we walked to the market and through the stalls, and together they bought something with a small amount of money. Then we all met back up in a grassy area to eat our snacks—some fruit and green beans.

## Activities

At the market, involve your children in helping to pick out fruits or vegetables of a particular color. We chose yellow, and they picked a pineapple and bananas. This activity could easily be done with a different color. Blue fruit salad? Green veggie salad?

### COLOR-Themed SNACK

## What to Do

1. Back at home or in the classroom, prepare your area and wash everyone's hands. Lay out a cutting board and knives.

2. Cut a slit across the bananas near the tip, and then children can work on peeling the bananas and putting the peels in the trash. This is an easy and excellent fine motor project for little fingers.

3. Then, together, slice the bananas. This is optional and depends on your comfort level. With help, close supervision, and a dull knife our toddlers were able to slice the bananas. Add the pieces to the bowl, and let the children take turns mixing.

4. A grown-up will need to slice the pineapple.

**Materials**

Fruits or vegetables of one color
Dull knives
Cutting boards

## New FRUIT Exploration

Sometimes we forget that to young children even simple things like a piece of fruit are a curiosity to be explored. At the farmers' market have the children help you pick out some unfamiliar fruits.

**Materials**

New or unfamiliar fruit
Knife (adult use only)

## What to Do

1. At home or in the classroom, rinse the fruit and sit at the table with your children.

2. Offer them the whole fruit to feel, look at, and smell. Describe with them or for them what they sense. "How does it feel on your hand?" "That scratchy part surprised you!"

3. Encourage them to smell the fruit or look closely if they don't do this on their own.

4. Then cut it open or peel it in front of them, and offer them a taste. Talk about what you are tasting and how the inside looks and feels different from the outside. This type of rich and respectful language will not only help to expand their vocabulary and make sense of what they are experiencing, but it also validates their reactions and observations. Something that seems silly or odd to us should still be respected, as it is the child's opinion. Showing openness to their ideas, whatever they are, will help them feel confident in communicating their perspectives to you and will further cement your relationship as one of support and care.

# Post Office

Everyone loves to get mail, and the post office is where mail happens. Write a letter, fill a box, or create a card, then address it together, and head to the post office. Look for the mail trucks and talk about the ones you see in your neighborhood. Consider purchasing the stamps there and applying them at the post office. Take turns putting things in the mailbox, and talk about where the mail will go next.

For groups, call ahead to your local post office and ask if they are willing to give you a behind-the-scenes tour. We did this with a group of children aged two to six when I was living in a smaller town, and the postal employees showed us the mailroom, answered questions, and let us climb in a mail truck.

**BRING**

Make sure you have one thing to mail per child.
Address everything and talk about what they will do when they get there, before you head to the post office.

**CONSIDER**

For children who are sensitive to noise, the mail room can be a little loud and crowded.

## DIY Mailbox

A simple mailbox can also be a great addition to a writing area.

### What to Do

1. Find a cardboard box, and cut a mail slot on one side. A big box that resembles a post office mailbox is ideal, but really any box will do.

**Materials**
Cardboard box
Scissors (adult use only)
Blue paint
Paintbrushes

2. Invite your children to help you paint the box blue like the post office mailbox. If you live in a country where the mailboxes are a different color, such as red, then paint the box that color.

3. When it is dry, place the mailbox in your play space with a mail carrier bag—any purse with a strap will do—and some letters to send.

Tip: Save the return envelopes you get with bills, for your pretend post office play.

## ABC Match Mail

Practice matching the letters of the alphabet while you pretend to be a mail carrier.

### What to Do

1. Create "mailboxes" around the house or classroom (simple cardboard boxes or any container will do) and attach a letter (A, B, C, etc.) to each.

**Materials**
Small cardboard boxes or other small containers
Envelopes
Marker

2. Label several envelopes with corresponding letters.

3. Have the children pretend to be the mail carrier who will deliver the mail by matching the letter on the envelope to the letter on the mailbox.

# Hardware Store

Children who are interested in tools, construction, and how things work will love the hardware store. If visiting with a class, this field trip works best if you divide into smaller groups. Small, cramped aisles could be overwhelming with a large group of toddlers who love to touch things.

**BRING** — Giving each child a list of the supplies you need or a copy of the scavenger hunt (see activity) is helpful in keeping the children's hands and minds occupied.

**CONSIDER** — Having a purpose to your trip is helpful. In my case, a small group of six two-year-olds visited the hardware store. We were working on a spring birdhouse project, and along with a parent volunteer at school, I took the six children to the hardware store a few blocks away to purchase the wood and a few other supplies we would need. Later, I did a similar project with my own twins.

**Most hardware stores have small hammers that are perfect for little woodworkers.**

# Activities

## Montessori 3 LESSON with TOOLS

The Montessori three-period lesson is a simple way to learn new vocabulary. This type of lesson, used in programs that follow the methods of Maria Montessori, can be used for introducing all sorts of new vocabulary and information to toddlers. This lesson with tools is just one example. Follow the same three steps below with any set of new words you wish to teach your child or small group.

### What to Do

Prepare by laying out the objects (tools in this case) that your children don't yet know. Then follow these three steps:

### Materials
3-5 tools

1. Identifying Objects. Pick up a tool. Let the children handle it while saying the name of the object several times. Continue with the other tools.

2. Association and Recognition. Ask a child to show you the correct object by pointing or bringing it to you as you say the name. If she can't do this yet, go back to step one. Once she correctly identifies the objects, move on.

3. Recall. Ask the child to recall what she has learned. Point to a tool and ask the child, "What is this?" If your child can't remember, return to step 2.

## GOLF TEE Hammering

This hammering activity develops children's eye-hand coordination skills.

### What to Do

1. Head outside and find a patch of dirt you don't mind damaging a little.

2. Gather some golf tees and child-size hammers for a simple hammering exercise.

### Materials
Golf tees
Child-size hammers

3. Hammer the golf tees into the ground a little way to get your children started. Then offer the children child-size hammers and let them hammer away.

Printmaking and painting with different tools is a fun way to create. Painting with a small hammer is also a way to practice the hammer motion and develop motor strength.

# HAMMER
## Painting

## What to Do

1. Pour the paint on a tray or nonbreakable plate, and lay out child-size hammers. Tape a large piece of paper to the ground or a tabletop. Invite your toddlers to paint.

2. Have them dip their tools into the paint and then make a print on their paper.

3. Repeat the process as desired.

### Materials
Child-size tools
Paper
Plate or tray
Paint
Painter's or duct tape

# Hardware Store Scavenger Hunt

Search for the items below when you visit the hardware store. You can always add or remove those you would prefer younger toddlers not find, such as nuts and bolts. Toddlers often want to "taste" anything they can find, and these small parts are a choking hazard.

Screws
Nuts and bolts
Lightbulbs
Hammer

Screwdriver
Protective eyewear
Hardware store worker
Keys

Light switches
Doorknob

# Map Walk

Although our world is largely dependent on smartphones and navigation devices when it comes to finding our way, I still believe it is important for young children to learn how to read a map. The first time I found myself underground in a subway station with no cell service, I was incredibly thankful for my map-reading skills. The ability to read maps also develops visual skills and navigational skills.

- You can start by making a simple map of your block or your favorite park (markers and white paper work great for this). Older toddlers who are beginning to understand that a picture can stand for a real-life item will start to be able to navigate a map.

- Draw out a map and then make a game out of it. I like to hide things and then have my children look for them using the map (see the Snack Map Hunt activity).

- You can also draw a wiggling path on your map and follow it together, labeling the things on the map that you are passing. The idea is to get outside, practice navigating, and practice the concept of things in print representing other ideas (an important preliteracy skill).

**BRING** Pack a stuffed animal or something else to hide, plus your map. Magnifying glasses can also be a fun addition.

**CONSIDER** Use the map together the first time or two to help teach the children how to recognize symbols and to navigate.

This is a great opportunity to learn new terms, so try to discuss some common vocabulary related to map reading.

## SNACK
### Map Hunt

This is one of our all-time favorite and most repeated activities. The process indoors is the same as an outdoor map walk but on a smaller scale.

## What to Do

1. Draw a map of the room. Prepare a simple snack such as a bowl with crackers, then hide the snack and indicate its position with a star.

2. Give the map to your toddlers to use to navigate to their snack. This is super easy to do and works on the same skills as a map walk.

3. For groups, you should have one map per group of four to five toddlers. For younger toddlers, the maps should be more basic and of smaller spaces. This activity is likely best for older toddlers or multiage groups.

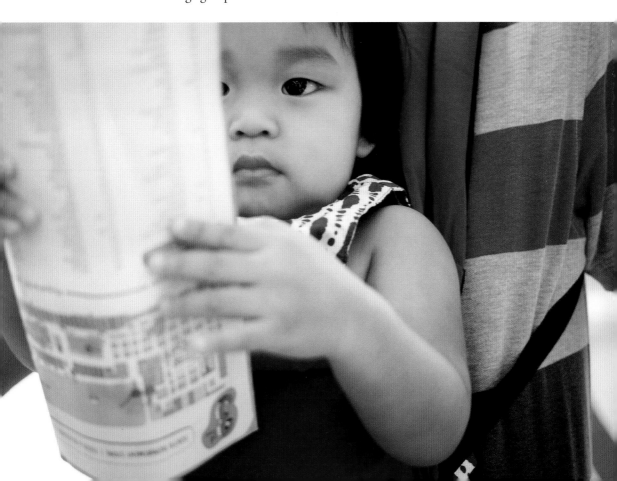

# LINE ART with YARN and Glue

Basic maps are generally a bunch of lines put together to represent something. Make a line picture (a map if you are working with older toddlers, or just line art) using yarn and glue.

## What to Do

1. Cut the yarn to various lengths. Encourage your children to help you with the cutting.

2. Then have them glue the yarn onto the paper or canvas. We like using colorful yarn, but you can also use a lighter color and then paint it the next day once the glue has dried. This adds a whole new dimension to the art.

### Materials

Thick paper or canvas
Yarn
Child-safe scissors
Glue

---

As I mentioned, learning that a picture can represent something is an important preliteracy skill. It is the foundation for understanding that letters and words can represent an idea or story. Help your children to master this idea by doing a picture-to-object match. You can easily make your own.

# Match PICTURE to OBJECT

## What to Do

1. Take photos of a bunch of objects around your house or classroom (clip art would also work), and print them out.

2. Place the photos next to a basket of the objects.

3. Demonstrate to your children how to lay out a picture and then search for the image that matches. To make this more difficult for older toddlers, hide the objects around the room so they have to find them first and then match them to the pictures.

### Materials

Camera
Printer
Variety of objects, typically in one group (animals, vehicles, kitchen utensils, etc.)
Basket or other container

# Photo Walk

Young children love to imitate behavior, so if they see you taking lots of pictures, they will want to take pictures as well. This might seem daunting, but I have had very successful photo walks with three to six toddlers.

- Start with a little instruction on how to use whatever camera is available. Having one camera per child is very helpful!
- Cameras that need a light touch to only one button on the back are the easiest to use for toddlers, but others can work as well.
- Teach the children how to hold the camera, where to look, and how to capture the image.
- Once they have had a little time to practice, go on your walk.

**BRING**  Pack one camera per child. You might also pack a notepad and pen for you to take notes.

**CONSIDER**  Parents are often willing to donate old cameras and cell phones if you work at a school or center. Old smartphones can often still take photos without needing a service plan.

**NOTICE**  Encourage them to stop and take pictures of whatever interests them. Your walk can take place anywhere: the neighborhood, inside your school, on a playground, on a hiking trail, etc.

# Activities

## Photo BOOK

Once you return from your walk, involve the toddlers as much as possible in bringing the photos from their cameras into their hands.

### Materials
Camera
Printer
Paper
Marker
Glue
Hole punch and rings
   (or yarn or ribbon)
Index cards or card stock
Clear contact paper (optional)

### What to Do

1. Download the photos, then pick a certain number of favorites and print them out.

2. Make a simple photo book using one of the processes described on page 7.

3. Once the photos are attached to the pages, encourage the children to dictate information about their photos to you to write on the pages. Let them share their photo books with a friend or classmate.

## HOUSE (or CLASSROOM) Photo Hunt

Toddlers love look-and-find books and hunting-for-things games. This is a simple one to do yourself.

### Materials
Photos of familiar objects
The actual objects

### What to Do

1. Take photos of various items around your house or classroom, and move the items to places where they might not normally be found. Prepare at least a couple per child, more depending on the age of the children and length of time you have to play.

2. Then, tell your toddlers that some items have been misplaced and you need their help finding them. The photos you hand the children are their assignments.

3. Invite them to help you hunt for the missing items and return them to their rightful places. The younger the child, the more obvious your clues should be.

# Baby Walk

**M**ost young children go through a phase where they enjoy caring for baby dolls. They cart them around, feed them, and put them to bed. While our twins were in this phase, we started going for baby walks. This meant one of two things: either they would push their babies in a baby stroller around our neighborhood (our favorite!), or I would use large swaddling blankets to tie the babies to their chests like an infant carrier and we would take them on adventures.

Large, thin swaddle blankets work best. The method that worked best for me was to fold the blanket in a triangle, tuck the baby doll in the middle of the triangle, loop the longer ends over the toddler's shoulders, and crisscross on her back. Tie it in the front.

**BRING**    Pack a doll or stuffed animal of the children's choice along with large swaddling blankets.

The children should also wear good shoes for walking.

**CONSIDER**    This activity followed our children's interests and added a fun element to our adventures. For example, we would take a hike with our babies and stop at various points to explain things to our dolls or "help them see things." You could say, "Let's show your baby the mailbox!" or "Do you think your baby wants to look at the flowers?" or "Can you tell your baby about what you see?" This is a fun way to develop language and support curiosity.

# Activities

## Baby Food TASTE Test

Toddlers are often interested in everything a baby does. They are curious about what they did as a baby and/or curious about what a younger sibling is doing now. A baby food taste test is a fun oral sensory experiment that supports this interest.

### Materials

Jars of baby food
Spoons

### What to Do

1. Gather some jars of baby food. Try to get a variety of textures, flavors, and colors.

2. One by one, offer your toddlers a test. Look at each food first, talk about the color, and guess what it might be or what it might taste like.

3. Have a taste, and then discuss your opinions.

4. Once you have tried them all, perhaps enjoy the rest of your favorite.

## BABY Play PROPS

Offering a basket of baby play props in your play space is a great way to extend play.

### What to Do

1. Gather some baby props for play. Try to make these as realistic as possible. Perhaps some children have siblings they can borrow a few things from or you have some baby stuff left over from their infancy. (Tip: Preemie diapers are often a perfect size for baby dolls!)

2. Consider modeling for your toddlers one of the items from the basket with a doll or stuffed animal. You might pick up a stuffed bear and say, "You are crying. Are you hungry? Let's try some of this food," and model how to feed your bear jarred food.

### Materials

Baby props—bought or donated (rattle, baby-food jar, small spoon, bottle, diaper-change supplies)
Toy babies or stuffed animals

# STRETCH
## with our
# BABIES

Mama-baby workouts are growing more popular and are a fun way for little ones to get active with their baby dolls as well. This activity supports your toddlers' gross motor development, and it's fun!

## Materials
1 doll per toddler

## What to Do

Find a big empty space and make sure each toddler has a baby.

Pick a doll to pretend with and get into acting as though it is a real baby. You can do this any way you wish, but we usually start with this basic routine.

1. Hold your doll in your hands, and lift it up high to the sky.
2. Lean to one side and then the other, still holding your doll.
3. Now reach down to your toes, and place your baby on the floor in front of you.
4. Bend forward and make a bridge with your arms touching the ground in front of you.
5. Come forward and say hi to your baby.
6. Press forward again.
7. Move down to your tummy on the mat, and as you lean up on your arms, play peekaboo with your baby.
8. Sit back on your heels.
9. Come to a seated position, and tickle your baby's tummy.

# Spotlight on Walks

The simplest adventures are right outside your door. Toddlers are interested in the world. What's nearby? Remember, everything is interesting to a toddler. Most children this age can walk about a mile. Brainstorm what is within a half mile that they might find intriguing. We have walked to see trees, flowers, and fire hydrants. You can see more ideas in the box at right, but the most important part about toddler walks is to focus on your toddlers' interests.

Go at their pace. Follow their interests. Answer their questions. Label things they point to while you explore.

## Extra Ideas for Walks

Car Walk
Bug Walk
Color Walk
Flower Color Walk
Big and Little Walk
Follow the Leader Walk
Signs of Fall Walk
Bird-Watching Walk
Leaf Walk

# Counting Walk

**W**hen our children reached the age of constantly counting (often incorrectly) everything around them, we headed outside for our first counting walk. Before we left, we wrote out a list of things they thought we could find outside, such as trees, cars, picnic tables, and bikes. We gathered the camera and their notebooks and markers. I guided them a little, but for the most part they chose the things for me to write/draw on the page. When we got outside, we checked the list and headed off in search of the first thing: trees. We counted all the trees we could see, and then I wrote it on our chart and encouraged them to "write" about it in their journals. Once they were satisfied, we moved on to the next thing. At times, one of them was more interested than the other, and I followed that child's lead.

**BRING**
It helps if each child has a clipboard or notebook for her counting list and a string to tie her pen to the clipboard (keeps it from getting lost).
They will each need a marker or pen to mark off found items.
Consider taking a camera along on your walk too.

**NOTICE**
Do not feel forced to finish your list or count only things on the list. Use the list as a starting point and follow your children's lead.

# Activities

## Count AROUND the HOUSE

Repetition is the hallmark of the infant/toddler years. They will want to do things again and again, and while you might not want or be able to go for a counting walk every day, you can probably do it on a smaller scale. Go on a counting walk around the house.

### Materials
Paper
Markers
Clipboards (optional but helpful)

### What to Do

1. Make a list, like you did for your adventure, of things to count. For example, count windows, doors, beds, people, etc.

2. Then head off to count around the house. You can consider doing this on an even smaller scale. Stick to one room. How many spoons are in the kitchen? How many appliances? How many gallons of milk?

3. Older toddlers can practice writing the numbers if they are interested. For younger toddlers, provide a box on the list next to the image of the item for them to just cross off or color after they have counted.

## DIY Counting Cards with STICKERS

Make these counting cards for your next counting walk, or tuck them in your diaper bag for the next time you are waiting somewhere.

### What to Do

1. Write the numerals 1–5 on five index cards.

2. Stick the corresponding number of stickers on each card.

3. On the back, tape or glue a photo with the corresponding number of people or objects.

4. Laminate with contact paper to make them sturdier.

### Materials
Index cards
Stickers
Glue stick or tape
Photos
Contact paper
Scissors
Marker or crayon

5. When your children are interested, practice identifying the number and counting the stickers and people. Encourage them to count using one extended finger, and model counting slowly one by one. It takes a while for children to gain an understanding of one-to-one correspondence. Practice with them using different materials to help them gain mastery.

# GATHER and COUNT: Our 10 Things

This almost zero prep activity is a great way to practice counting to ten (or whatever number you want) with children.

## Materials

Large piece of paper or cardboard

Markers

## What to Do

1. Young children learn best through interactive, hands-on play and activity that involves using the senses and working cooperatively with others. Invite your toddlers to help you count ten things. This activity helps your children build many skills, including cognitive development as they explore numbers. We did this part of the activity outside, but it would work in a classroom or playroom as well.

2. Grab a big piece of paper or cardboard, and write "Our 10 Things" or something similar.

3. Tell the children that you all need to work together to find ten things and bring them to the paper.

4. You can divide this up however you want. For instance, if you have two children, have them each look for five things.

5. If you have some older and some younger toddlers, give the older children a bigger number to gather and the younger children something simple such as two.

6. As the items are gathered, spread them out on the paper. Count together to mark progress and figure out how many more you need or whether you have too many.

7. This is optional, but we decided we wanted to save our collection. To do this, we used washi tape to stick the found items to the paper. Then we used a marker to trace the things we couldn't tape, such as watering cans.

# Bakery

Who doesn't enjoy a trip to the bakery? The smell of bread. The delicious pastries. You can make a trip to the bakery as basic or in-depth as you want.

A simple trip to the bakery offers opportunities for language development, sensory input, and opportunities to learn about the roles and processes of a bakery. You can also ask your local bakery if they would be willing to answer your children's questions or give them a tour. Many small businesses are open to an idea like this if you ask and are willing to come at a less busy time.

**BRING** — Pack some cash so your toddlers can make the purchases. Encourage them to help order and pay if they have enough language to do so.

**CONSIDER** — A wide range of options, say an entire case filled with cookies and pastries, can be overwhelming to a toddler. Plan ahead for two choices that would work well and appeal to your toddlers, and then let them pick between just those things.

Make sure to consider food allergies and dairy restrictions before going to a bakery. Dairy and egg allergies can be especially tricky with baked goods.

# FLOUR
## Sensory Table

In this super-fun sensory table activity, children get to put their hands right into the materials for baking.

## What to Do

1. Consider doing this activity outside because the flour does tend to get everywhere. Fill your sensory tub with flour. (I used 8 five-pound bags.)

2. Place some spoons, shakers filled with jimmies or glitter, bowls, whisks, etc. in the sensory tub.

3. Invite your children to come cook.

### Materials
Sensory table or bin
8 five-pound bags of flour
Basic cooking tools:
   spoons, whisks, bowls
Shakers filled with jimmies
   or glitter

# CUPCAKE
## Playdough
# INVITATION

This invitation is simple to create and so much fun.

## What to Do

1. Set out some playdough, cupcake wrappers, and sequins as an invitation on a table. Most toddlers don't need much additional instruction, but if your children seem unsure, prompt them a little by asking, "What could you make?" or model how to start a cupcake.

2. Pretend you are actually baking the cupcake or that it just came out of the oven: "Ouch! Hot!"

3. Enjoy the pretend-play aspect and your toddlers will have more fun with it as well. Your toddlers will also be building fine motor development skills as they play with these materials.

### Materials
Playdough
Silicone cupcake
   wrappers (paper
   wrappers work but
   are less reusable)
Sequins

# Park

**M**ost children spend at least some time at the local park. Other open green spaces work as well. Parks, however, are a great community space for gross motor activity and fresh air.

Make sure to pack sunscreen and have everyone wear weather-appropriate clothing.

To add a little extra fun to your next park outing, you could:

- go on a scavenger hunt.
- take some sand toys to play in the sand.
- create an obstacle course with the play equipment.
- play hide and seek.

Whatever you do, try to follow your toddlers' interests to see what they most enjoy doing at the park.

## Stuffed ANIMAL Park Play

Make an extra trip to the park this week, or play this game on a backyard or school playground slide.

### Materials
1 stuffed animal per toddler

### What to Do

1. Bring your stuffed animals or baby dolls along, and send them down the slide. This is great for little ones who are interested in caring for animals or babies. It supports their interest in role playing the parent role. It also adds a little gross motor challenge for young toddlers.

## Shades of GREEN Paintings

If your park has some green space, you might talk about the color green. Our younger toddlers were always fascinated by grass.

### What to Do

1. Pick some grass at the park or in your yard, and take it inside to your art table.

2. Pull out some crayons and markers of different shades of green, or mix white and green paint together to explore different shades of green. Ask the children, Which one looks the most like the grass? Which shade of green do you like the best? What else can you find around the house (or room) that is green?

### Materials
Paper
Crayons, markers in
   shades of green
White and green paint
Paintbrushes (if painting)

# Library

I hope, I hope that you already visit your public library. Libraries are incredible resources for books, information, and story times and for meeting other parents or caregivers of young children. Did I mention the books? Aim to add the library to your calendar at least once a month. Get your toddlers in the habit of finding new books to love. Fill your home with new books on a regular basis to inspire reading, explore different genres and authors, learn about topics, and encourage an early love of literacy. If you work in child care, check with the local library on story-time policies. Most welcome programs with low teacher-to-child ratios.

**BRING** Make sure to pack your library card and a big, sturdy bag for books.

**CONSIDER** Use your library's online system to request books in advance. This way you have some books ready to be checked out. I typically do a combination of letting my children pick books and requesting some books on topics they are learning about or that have been recommended. This way I'm not trying to look for books while I'm keeping an eye on the children. I can spend our time browsing with them, reading to them, or supervising play.

# Activities

## Make Your Own BOOK

As I have mentioned, there are many ways to make your own books. I make them often for new topics of interest, field trips, and about my toddlers.

### Materials
Paper
Markers
Camera and printer
Hole punch and rings
  (or yarn or ribbon)
Index cards or card stock
Clear contact paper (optional)

### What to Do

For younger toddlers, you might want to make a word book. Go around your home or classroom and see what they point to. To start:

1. Snap a picture.

2. Then create a book with the photo and the word labeling the item on each page. See directions for making your book on page 7.

3. Read the book together over and over.

More ideas? Create a book of faces and emotion words. Create a book about your family. Create a book based on one of your favorites from the library. Laura Numeroff's series that includes books such as *What Mommies Do Best/What Daddies Do Best* was fun inspiration for us.

## PLAY LOOK and FIND with Parts of a BOOK

Take some time during a read aloud to talk about the parts of the book.

### What to Do

1. Before you begin reading, show your toddlers the different parts of the book.

2. Can your children find the front? the back? the spine? the title? the author? an illustration? the words? a library barcode? Depending on your children's ages, this can be short or more detailed.

### Materials
Any picture book

3. With young toddlers, I would start with just two or three parts of the book until they have those mastered. Get in the habit of reading the title and the author and occasionally discussing the parts of the book.

Reenacting a story is an important preliteracy skill. Children are often unable to do this independently until they are closer to kindergarten, but you can lay the groundwork now.

# ACT OUT a STORY

## What to Do

1. Read a story that the children know well, and then act it out together with yourselves and/or stuffed animals. If they like a story about a truck, find a truck and act out the story together. If they like *Good Night, Gorilla* or another classic, get creative about how you can reenact the tale.

### Materials
A favorite picture book
Stuffed animals to represent main characters

2. One of my favorites to act out with toddlers is *Good Night, Gorilla*. The brief, repetitive text and simple story make it easy to remember and reenact.

Tip: I have found that toddlers understand this best if you read the story or at least review the pictures along with your retelling the first time. Look at a page and act out what is happening. Then move to the next page.

**Big trucks, loud noises, community helpers**

Is it really any surprise that young children are so often fascinated by vehicles? They seem larger than life. We often observe toddlers playing with toy trucks. They imitate the vrooming noises and drive trucks around on the carpet. In the following adventures, you will discover new ways to expand this interest and affirm toddlers' fascination with these awesome vehicles.

# Vehicles

# Fire Station

**D**o your toddlers ask you to read books about fire trucks over and over again? Do they pretend to be firefighters? Do they point out out every fire truck they spot on the road? If the answer is yes, the fire station is a great field trip for you! Talk to your toddlers beforehand about some of the things you might see or hear: the fire trucks, firefighters, the loud siren, and the uniforms and masks.

There are two ways to go about a fire-station visit. If you have a group of toddlers, you can call the fire station and arrange a visit. The firefighters will show you their gear and their trucks and do a little presentation. In most communities you can also just visit your neighborhood fire station. Unless the firefighters are called away or busy cleaning up after a call, they are usually very happy to take some time to talk to your toddlers. I have always been impressed by their kindness and willingness to talk with children.

**BRING** | Pack a camera and take pictures. We spent a lot of time referring to the pictures of our trip in the weeks to follow.

You might also pack a list of questions your toddlers have for the visit.

**CONSIDER** | If you have children in your group who are particularly sensitive to loud noises, either prepare them for the siren before it is turned on or talk to the firefighters about skipping that part of their tour.

## Activities

# Visit a FIRE HYDRANT and Investigate It Up CLOSE

This is another mini-adventure to go with your trip to the fire station.

## What to Do

1. Head outside and find your nearest fire hydrant.

2. Take pictures of the fire hydrant.

3. Talk about the different parts of the fire hydrant.

4. Hypothesize about where and how you think the hose would hook up. Listen—What are they noticing? What are they wondering?

5. If they are interested, have your toddlers draw pictures of the fire hydrant. Compare the fire hydrants to one shown in one of the firefighter books on your shelf.

### Materials
Cameras
Journals
Colored pencils, markers

# Practice STOP, DROP, and ROLL

This exercise is simple and can be done anywhere.

## What to Do

1. Find an open space.

2. Pretend you have caught fire, and then act out how to stop, drop, and roll. Be dramatic as you act it out.

3. Then invite your children to practice with you. Act it out a few times to practice.

4. If you want, play another game but occasionally shout, "Fire!" and have them stop what they are doing, drop, and roll. For example, play tag, ride bikes, or simply walk in circles, and then call out, "Fire!" to practice some more.

### Materials
None

# Construction Site

**D**o you have children who love construction trucks? In that case, nothing is better than seeing these vehicles in action. Many months of the year, you can find construction happening somewhere. Scout your area ahead of time, or pay attention to where construction is happening. Find a site that is away from traffic, such as a building or a new park. Head out to watch the trucks in action. Watch them scoop, dig, and dump.

**BRING** — Pack a camera and a book of construction vehicles to help you identify what you're seeing.

**NOTICE** — Pay attention to the questions your children ask. Help them to notice what the different trucks are doing.

## Activities

Heavy work is important for the development of young children. This means carrying, moving, and pushing heavy (to them) things. After watching big trucks work, pretend you are dump trucks!

## CARRYING Heavy LOADS

### Materials
Heavy (for toddlers) boxes, blocks, logs, etc.

### What to Do

1. Find some heavy (for a toddler) boxes, logs, blocks, or whatever is available, and tell your toddlers that your room or play area is a building site.

2. The dump truck's assignment is to move the items from one space to the other so that the building can be built. Can they help you?

# Construction TRUCK Paint

This is not a new activity for toddlers. I wish I knew where I first learned this activity, but I imagine it was early on in my child-care-teacher days. This one is adaptable for any vehicle including trains, cars, planes, and construction trucks.

## What to Do

1. Tape a large piece of paper on a tabletop or the floor. I recommend one large tabletop-size paper per three to five toddlers.

2. Make sure each toddler has at least one car. Two is better.

3. To paint, your toddlers will run their trucks in the paint and then drive them across the paper, making paint tracks.

4. Have some fun with truck noises as they drive around.

## Materials

Large paper
Plastic trucks (either washable or old ones you don't mind being painted)
Paint

# Construction SITE Small WORLD

Small worlds or sensory bins can be another way to invite pretend play. While toddlers generally prefer whole-body pretending, such as cooking food in a pretend kitchen instead of having little people in a dollhouse cook food, there are some things, such as trains or trucks, that can work well on a smaller stage.

## What to Do

1. Create a small version of a construction site with sand or dirt as the foundation. Add rocks and construction trucks.

2. Give your toddlers various things to scoop and dig.

3. Leave it as an invitation to play for your children to find. Consider adding toy people or a new building material such as blocks later in the week.

## Materials

Sensory table or tub
Sand or dirt
Rocks
Toy construction trucks

# Car Walk

If you cannot think of enough transportation activities for your car-loving toddlers, this adventure is for you. Toddlers love to take walks, so this activity combines their love of walks and cars. Start by picking a car of a certain color to look for first. Let each toddler have a chance to pick. From there, alternate between looking for that color and labeling the color of cars you see. If your children are more interested in the types of vehicles, look for that. Who can spot a truck? an SUV? a Jeep?

**BRING** ▶ Pack your camera and a nonfiction book about vehicles.

**CONSIDER** ▶ The trick is to find a spot to watch where you aren't so close to the road you will feel nervous the whole time, but not so far away that you can't see much. Grassy spots are usually good.

## Activities

## CAR COLOR Match

Matching is an early math skill that toddlers can master with this activity.

### What to Do

1. Place cars or trucks of different colors and some squares of fabric or construction paper in a basket together.

2. When your toddlers are interested, encourage them to explore the materials.

### Materials

Cars or trucks of different colors
Fabric or construction paper in matching colors
Basket

3. After a bit, if they haven't done so on their own, invite them to help you match the cars to the same color squares.

4. Drive the trucks to their matches to have more fun.

# CAR
## Passing

**Practice taking turns and develop motor skills by passing cars back and forth.**

## What to Do

1. Spread out however many people you have (two to four is best) and pass a car among each other.

2. Make sure to "vroom!" as you pass the car to your toddlers.

3. Then encourage them to pass the car to the next person.

### Materials
Toy car (one per small group)

# Vehicles Booklist

Children who love vehicles will enjoy these books. There are so many to choose from, but these are some of my favorites.

*Count on the Subway* by Paul DuBois Jacobs and Jennifer Swender

*Diggers Go* by Steve Light

*Freight Train* by Donald Crews

*Good Night Engines* by Denise Dowling Mortensen

*The Noisy Airplane Ride* by Mike Downs

*Planes* by Byron Barton

*The Racecar Alphabet* by Brian Floca

*Red Car, Red Bus* by Susan Steggall

*This Is the Firefighter* by Laura Godwin

*Toot Toot Beep Beep* by Emma Garcia

*Train* by Elisha Cooper

*Trains* by Gail Gibbons

*Wheels on the Bus* by Raffi

# Car Wash

Part of owning a car is caring for it: filling it with gas, repairing it, and washing it. The car wash can be a fun field trip for the sights and sounds.

**BRING** — Pack lovies or stuffed animals in case they get nervous.

**CONSIDER** — The car wash can be overwhelming. Prepare your toddlers for what they will see and hear. Explain to them the process and what the different machines are doing. Consider demonstrating with a toy car.

If your toddlers are afraid of the dark or loud noises, skip this adventure until they are a little older.

## Activities

### Toy CAR WASH

Wash your toy cars.

**Materials**

2 shallow bins or tubs
Water
Washcloths
Washable cars
Soap

#### What to Do

1. Fill both bins with water. Add soap to one bin.

2. Drive your car through the soapy bin.

3. Then drive your car through the rinse-water bin.

4. Dry it off. Repeat!

5. Consider making an assembly line, and giving each person a job at the car wash. For younger toddlers this will likely resemble water play. That is okay. The language building and sensory experiences are more important than the actual clean car.

# Tire RUBBING

This activity is based on the idea of a bark or leaf rubbing.

## Materials

Paper

Crayons

Real car tire (see description for alternatives)

## What to Do

1. The idea is to get up close to a tire and look at the pattern so that you can talk about why tires have treads.

2. Encourage your toddlers to feel the tire (yes, they will have to wash their hands afterward) and experience the texture.

3. Show the children how to place a piece of paper on the tire and rub a crayon across it.

4. If you want to make a rubbing but can't use an actual tire, consider making tracks instead by either doing car painting again, driving cars in playdough, or taking the tires off of larger trucks (such as the ones you put in your sandbox), and making tracks with paint.

# LOOK at a CAR Up Close

Visit a real car today, yours or someone else's. Ask first, of course!

## What to Do

1. Walk around the car with the children.

2. Listen to what they notice or ask them, "What do you see?"

3. Label the different parts (print out an online guide if you aren't a car part expert), compare and contrast two cars, or compare one in real life with one in a book.

4. If your toddlers are interested, invite them to take photos or draw a picture.

## Materials

A real car or other vehicle

Camera (optional)

# Bus Ride

Have you ever gone on a bus ride with a young child? Not out of necessity or even to get somewhere in particular, but for the experience? If you have children who love transportation, riding on something that goes should be a natural adventure for you to take. This is one of our all-time favorite adventures.

**BRING**  Pack exact change for the fare, a full diaper bag, and weather-appropriate clothing.

**CONSIDER**  City buses are typically accessible for the physically disabled. Check your local transit website for any details that will make your adventure go more smoothly.

Use the online transit website for your area to plan your trip. Make sure you know the route number and your stop, going both ways.

**NOTICE**  Our son went through a period when he was fascinated by buses. We sang "The Wheels on the Bus" all day long, and he drove around a little toy bus constantly. We read every version of *Wheels on the Bus* in book form that I could find. Taking him for a ride on a real bus was the perfect adventure. This was an easy, fun, and exciting adventure for a toddler and the perfect example of just how simple an early childhood field trip can be.

# Activities

## Sing Songs:
## WHEELS
## on the BUS

Sing "The Wheels on the Bus."

## What to Do

Sing the song together. Once you and your toddlers are familiar with the original, invent your own version with different animals, family members, etc.

| Materials |
| --- |
| **None** |

*The wheels on the bus go 'round and 'round,*
*'Round and 'round*
*'Round and 'round.*
*The wheels on the bus go 'round and 'round,*
*All day long.*

*The horn on the bus goes beep, beep, beep*
*Beep, beep, beep*
*Beep, beep, beep.*
*The horn on the bus goes beep, beep, beep,*
*All day long.*

*The wipers on the bus go swish, swish, swish*
*Swish, swish, swish*
*Swish, swish, swish.*
*The wipers on the bus go swish, swish, swish,*
*All day long.*

*The baby on the bus says, "Wah, wah, wah*
*Wah, wah, wah*
*Wah, wah, wah."*
*The baby on the bus says, "Wah, wah, wah,"*
*All day long.*

*The bell on the bus goes ding, ding, ding*
*Ding, ding, ding*
*Ding, ding, ding*
*The bell on the bus goes ding, ding, ding,*
*All day long.*

*The money on the bus (or in the box) goes clink, clink,*
*clink*
*Clink, clink, clink*
*Clink, clink, clink.*
*The money on the bus goes clink, clink, clink,*
*All day long.*

*The driver on the bus says, "Move on back*
*move on back, move on back."*
*The driver on the bus says, "Move on back,"*
*All day long.*

*The windows on the bus go up and down*
*Up and down*
*Up and down.*
*The windows on the bus go up and down,*
*All day long.*

*The mommy on the bus says, "Shush, shush, shush*
*Shush, shush, shush*
*Shush, shush, shush."*
*The mommy on the bus says, "Shush, shush, shush,"*
*All day long.*

*The people on the bus laugh, "Ha, ha, ha*
*Ha, ha, ha*
*Ha, ha, ha."*
*The people on the bus laugh, "Ha, ha, ha,"*
*All day long.*

# Paper Plate STEERING Wheels

Make pretend bus driver steering wheels.

## What to Do

1. Cut the middles out of sturdy paper plates, and then prepare a painting invitation.

2. Let your toddlers paint their plates whatever colors they choose.

3. Let the plates dry overnight, and then use them while you sing "The Wheels on the Bus" or on your pretend bus ride.

## Materials

Paper plates
Scissors (for adults)
Paint
Paintbrushes

# PRETEND Play BUS Ride

Go for a pretend bus ride with other toddlers, siblings, or stuffed animals.

## What to Do

1. Line up some chairs or hop on a long couch and pretend you are riding on a bus.

2. Try to include some of the steps you learned from your real bus ride, such as paying the driver, pulling the cord, waiting, watching out the window, etc.

3. Toddlers will often all want to play the same role. It is okay to have five drivers on your pretend bus. The focus on this activity is reenacting the things they saw and heard on your adventure. You want them to practice the new words and concepts about riding a bus that they learned.

4. You (or stuffed animals) can always play the roles of passengers or driver or whatever is not the currently desirable role.

## Materials

Chairs or other props
Stuffed animals (optional)
Your steering wheels (made earlier)

# Auto Parts Store

**A**n auto parts store is full of car parts and is a great place to break down the parts of the car and build vocabulary. Before you go, take a walk around a car, bus, or truck. Make a list of parts the children know. Write the word next to a photo of each part. Look for those inside the store and check them off your list.

**BRING**   Pack a pen and notepad to write a list of car parts and questions.

**CONSIDER**   Follow the children's lead. If they lose interest in your list, don't worry about it. Let them show you what they are curious about. You can also head back to the list later if you need to refocus or you can try again another time.

---

## Activities

### FIX Your Trike SHOP

This is another simple but fun pretend scenario for toddlers.

#### What to Do

1. Gather some toy tools and riding toys and set up a tricycle shop.

2. Make a sign together that says "Trike Repair Shop."

**Materials**
Toy tools
Bikes/trikes/riding toys
Poster board or construction
   paper
Marker

3. This pretend invitation might be less obvious to your toddlers than some, so ask if they can help repair riding toys. You may need to model for your toddlers by bringing a trike or wagon that is "broken" and asking them to fix it.

4. When it is fixed, make sure someone rides it to make sure it is fully repaired.

# Count the PARTS on Your VEHICLE

Take the list of car parts that you used at the auto shop (windows, steering wheel, etc.) and use it on your own family vehicle or a teacher's vehicle.

## What to Do

1. Go down the list and look for and count each item on your vehicle. For example, find the tires and count them.

2. Write that number next to the word and picture on your list. I know you already did this, but remember: repetition is good. In this case, it helps to cement the idea that all vehicles have similar parts.

### Materials

List of car parts
Vehicle
Pen or crayon

## —— Scavenger Hunt: Road ——

This is a good list of things to look for, such as signs and red or blue cars, when you and the children are walking near a road. If you think of something else they might like to search for, add it to your list.

| | | |
|---|---|---|
| Red car | Passenger | Delivery truck |
| Bus | Driver | Speed limit sign |
| Stop sign | Yellow car | Bicycle |
| Bus sign | Crosswalk | |

# Bridge

Our interest in bridges started with train bridges. Our twins would notice them when we were driving around our town. An interest in bridges does not have to be train related, however. Bridges are fun. You drive under them and over them. You can also walk over them!

**BRING** ▸ Pack binoculars and a camera to take photos for a related activity.

**CONSIDER** ▸ Talk about expectations and safety precautions before you go.

**NOTICE** ▸ Hopefully you have a bridge or two in your area. Go under and over bridges, repeating the words *under* and *over*. Let the children get up close to the bridge and explore what interests them. Our toddlers enjoyed running across the bridge and watching the water go under the bridge.

## Activities

### BRIDGE and TUNNEL Sort

This is a sorting and vocabulary-building exercise in one.

## What to Do

1. Print photos of bridges and tunnels from your walk or the internet.

2. Tape two large pieces of paper to a surface.

3. Write *Bridges* on one and *Tunnels* on the other (I also drew little pictures).

4. Place your photos in a basket and have tape on hand.

5. Ask your toddlers to help you sort. Show them the two charts, indicating the word and picture that indicates bridge or tunnel. Do the first one together. For example, "Let's look at the first picture that Charlie is holding. What do you see in the picture?" "Why do you think it is a bridge?" or "I agree. There are cars driving under it; it looks like a bridge to me too! Here's some tape. Can you attach it to the *Bridge* chart?"

6. If the example goes well, let them take the lead from there. If not, do more of them together. Try to use questions or shared thoughts to lead them to an answer, rather than just saying *right* or *wrong*. I have found referring to other pictures, either ones you have already charted or those in a book, to also be helpful. Use the vocabulary introduced on the bridge walk, including *bridge, tunnel, over, under, long, short*, and maybe some specific bridge types with older children.

# BALANCE
## Bridge
# WALKING

Pretend and move your bodies with this simple activity.

## What to Do

1. All you need is something to use as a pretend bridge (piece of rope, 2' x 4' piece of wood, wooden blocks, etc.). A chalk line can do in a pinch.

2. Draw a "river" on the ground with blue chalk, and then place your bridge across it as a balancing invitation.

3. Toddlers have only very basic balancing skills, so this low "bridge" is perfect for practicing.

# Sing & Play:
# LONDON BRIDGE

"London Bridge Is Falling Down" is a classic song and perfect for this themed activity.

## What to Do

With at least three people, play and sing at the same time. Two people are the bridge, holding their hands together like an arch or bridge. Everyone else goes under the bridge while the song is sung until it "all falls down." Make the "bridge" collapse on someone by bringing your arms down around the person. Sing the song, "London Bridge Is Falling Down."

*London Bridge is falling down*
*Falling down, falling down*
*London Bridge is falling down*
*My fair lady*

*Build it up with iron bars*
*Iron bars, iron bars*
*Build it up with iron bars*
*My fair lady*

*Iron bars will bend and break*
*Bend and break, bend and break*
*Iron bars will bend and break*
*My fair lady*

*Build it up with gold and silver*
*Gold and silver, gold and silver*
*Build it up with gold and silver*
*My fair lady*

*London Bridge is falling down*
*Falling down, falling down*
*London Bridge is falling down*
*My fair lady*

# Hot-Air Balloon Festival

**H**ot-air balloon festivals are fun, family-friendly affairs that happen around the United States and throughout the world. Sometimes there is a race involved and sometimes there is a more casual balloon lift, but regardless, it is fun. Honestly, it is a little hard to describe why I think these are so cool, but I assure you young children agree with me on this. For young children, the immense size of the balloons coupled with the diversity of splendid color amounts to a visual feast for the eyes.

This is one of the few adventures in this book that I have done only once and not with a larger group of toddlers. This is a logistics issue since the festivals in our area have always happened on a weekend. I have, however, done this once with my own children when they were younger toddlers, and despite it being a very cold January morning in Minnesota, we loved it so much that I had to include it here.

**BRING** Often these events happen in the morning, so dress for cooler temperatures. It takes a while for those balloons to inflate, so bundle your toddlers, and take some snacks for them to eat while they watch.

**CONSIDER** Even if you are a teacher and can't take your whole class to a festival, you could share information about it with your families.

**NOTICE** A hot-air balloon festival is a great place to learn new vocabulary, such as *balloon, basket, flame,* and much more.

## GLUE and YARN Collage

After festivals and parades, colors are often the first thing that come to my mind and the minds of my toddlers when we are discussing our experience: the bright blue balloon, the rainbow balloon. These collages are a celebration of the jumble of colors and ropes you might see.

## What to Do

### Materials

Placemat or table covering
Bottle or cup of glue
Paintbrushes
Bowl or basket
Colorful yarn
Black construction paper

1. Start with a simple glue exploration if your toddlers haven't played with glue before. Give them some paper and glue and let them explore.

2. Glue is a messy, thrilling experience for most little ones. For all glue projects with young children, allow them to play with it, stick and unstick things, smear it on their hands and paper. Eventually, the neat gluing that we do as adults will emerge, but first toddlers need to make a creative mess. Let them.

3. Once children are comfortable with glue, try adding things such as yarn to their exploration.

4. Remember that it is about the process. Gluing is a skill. Don't worry about what the picture looks like. Instead, comment on the process, help when they are frustrated, and give them space and time to explore.

5. Toddlers often do better with a cup of glue and a paintbrush rather than a bottle. This is not true of all toddlers, though, so experiment with what works for you and yours. This is a free exploration, process-oriented invitation to create. I insist that art materials stay at the art table, but otherwise the children generally have free rein. Paint with glue, dip string in the glue, and move string around their papers. Some string will stick but some won't. Your job is not to worry about the end product, but to sit with them or nearby. Support them if they have trouble, and comment and ask questions.

# BALLOON
## Hot-Air Gross
## Motor Activity

Follow this simple routine to move your bodies and re-tell the story from your hot-air balloon adventure.

**Materials**
None

## What to Do

1. Find an open space and have everyone remove socks and shoes, then spread out and sit on the floor.

2. Start to fill with air. Make the noise to add some fun, and slowly move upward until you are standing with your arms and legs outstretched. Now you are a large inflated balloon.

3. Stand with arms at your sides. Move legs together, arms to your sides, and move like people getting into the balloon. Arch your back and arms backward as you take off.

4. Airplane pose: Move to the floor on your stomach. Arch your backs and spread your arms out wide to imagine you are flying away into the sky.

5. Roll over onto your backs and relax. Take deep breaths and imagine you are floating back to the ground.

# Contact Paper
# and TISSUE
# Paper Hot-Air
# BALLOONS

I love collaborative art projects for giving toddlers time to create while working on their social skills.

## What to Do

1. Cut an oval shape out of contact paper, and prepare a large basket of tissue paper squares.

2. Tape the contact-paper oval sticky side up to a tabletop, and invite your toddlers to stick tissue paper to the oval.

3. If you have more than one toddler, make the oval larger for a fun, collaborative project.

4. When you are done, you have the colorful balloon portion for tomorrow's creation.

**Materials**
Contact paper
Tissue paper
Scissors (for adult use)
Masking tape
Basket

# Gas Station

Most vehicles don't run without gasoline, so gas stations are an important place for learning about vehicles.

While planning your visit, try to avoid rush hours and super-busy gas stations. Find one in a neighborhood, and visit on a weekday morning. You will be able to enjoy the trip more if you aren't worried about the constant stream of cars coming in and out.

**BRING**

If you are going with one toddler, stop by when you have time to walk your toddler through the process.

If you are going with a group, find a quieter station and talk to the station manager beforehand.

**CONSIDER**

Talk to your toddlers about the different steps to buying gasoline, such as how you know what buttons to push, what decisions you make, and where the payment goes, etc.

# Activities

## DIY Gas STATION

I learned to do this from my very first student-teaching experience. The center where I worked had several of these in the gym space and it was genius. The children were in love. It was so much fun that I have duplicated it in several settings since.

### What to Do

1. Gather a box or two that stands about 2–3 feet tall.

2. Attach a rope or bendable tube to one side of the box with duct tape.

3. Draw some simple gas station–like buttons and displays on a piece of card stock, and attach that to the box as well.

4. Invite your little ones to help pump gas into each other's bikes.

### Materials

Box (1 per 5 toddlers)
Rope or bendable tube
Duct tape
Markers
Card stock or construction paper

## OUT-OF-GAS Running GAME

This is a game to play outside with toddlers.

### What to Do

1. Give one or two children a "gas hose" (simple weather stripping, rope, or clear tubing works well), and tell them they are the gas attendants.

2. The other children (and you) pretend to be cars or trucks.

3. Drive around like a truck really fast at first and then slower and slower until you stop.

4. When you decide to stop/run out of gas, the attendants hurry over to fill you up with gas so you can start running fast again.

5. For older children who desire more of a goal, create a track. They start fast but have to stop by the time they end a lap. They wait to get refilled and then run again. The first person to loop a certain number of times wins.

### Materials

Weather stripping, rope, clear tubing

# Ordering BIG, MEDIUM, and LITTLE

Different-sized cars need different gas. This activity is a playful way to practice ordering things by size, a math concept.

## What to Do

1. Gather vehicles in a variety of sizes, and place them in a basket together.

2. Then create a pump station for each. Simple paper -towel rolls labeled *Big, Medium,* and *Little* do the trick.

3. Sort the vehicles you have into big, medium, and little and then pretend to give them gas. For younger toddlers, sort the vehicles into just two sizes: big and little.

### Materials

Variety of toy vehicles
Paper-towel tubes
Markers
Scissors (adult use)
Basket

# Spotlight on the Arts

Art is powerful. In the world of science, technology, engineering, and math (STEM) and test-driven education, the arts are often unfortunately overlooked. The art world and teachers are not giving up though, and many people encourage the incorporation of the arts into STEM curriculum, creating STEAM. I wholeheartedly concur.

When I was in grade school, I was fortunate to attend the art magnet school in my hometown. It no longer exists in its past form due to budget cuts, but when I was in elementary school it was an amazing place. Each regular grade teacher was required to have both a teaching degree and at least a minor in some form of art. This meant that the arts were regularly integrated into our learning. We also had weekly "specials" when we got more direct instruction in dance, art, music, and drama.

I don't consider myself to be above average creativity-wise, but thanks to my years there I feel like I have an above-average appreciation for the arts. All children should have the same opportunities to appreciate art and to be surrounded with opportunities to express themselves. Much like Loris Malaguzzi described in his beautiful poem "The Hundred Languages," I believe children should be offered a myriad of tools and methods to communicate their ideas and build knowledge. Art should be part of every child's day. Creative or dramatic play. Painting and drawing. Inventing stories. Listening to music. When art surrounds us and is incorporated into everything else we do, it becomes a powerful mediator of knowledge, a communication tool, and a supporter of emotional development.

What can you do? If you are artistically inclined, share your art form with your children. Play music for them on your guitar or piano, dance with them, put on plays together, or find time to create side by side. If you are less confident in your art skills, find others to inspire you both. Visit art museums and children's theaters. Find summer camps or family programs that introduce art skills. Experiment together with different materials. Try different things and see what interests your child the most. The beautiful thing about creativity is that there are no wrong answers.

# Train Ride

If your children spend hours driving around trains or building tracks, research your area for a train ride. Many communities have either a full-size restored train or a miniature children's train, or take your toddlers on an actual Amtrak, subway, or other commuter train. All will be fun for a train enthusiast.

**BRING**
Dress for the weather because trains are often open air, at worst, or not temperature controlled, at best.

You may want to pack a camera to take pictures of things that interest your toddlers as well as a list of questions your children have about trains.

**CONSIDER**
Train rides can be tricky for children in wheelchairs. Although many trains are accessible, some are only accessible in a limited number of stations. Scope this out with the help of your transit office beforehand if needed.

**NOTICE**
Pay attention to all the details, and listen to what questions your children ask. This will help you understand what part of the train ride or trains in general interests them and how you can expand their learning through play.

# Activities

## TRAIN Pretend Play

A couch or group of chairs can easily become a train for imaginative toddlers.

**Materials**
Couch or chairs
Paper
Scissors (adult only)
Markers

### What to Do

1. Make some simple tickets with paper, scissors, and markers.

2. The setup for the train is the same as the bus. I typically use rows of chairs to make either.

3. Once everything is ready, take turns playing the different roles on the train ride.

4. Help your toddlers remember the words for *engineer, conductor,* and *passenger* to practice their language learning.

## FREIGHT TRAIN Color Sort

*Freight Train* by Donald Crews is one of the best train books for toddlers. It is simple, beautiful, and a great lesson in colors. Practice color recognition and sorting skills with this simple activity.

**Materials**
Freight cars
Construction paper
Scissors

### What to Do

1. Gather some freight cars from your train set.

2. Cut small squares of paper in different colors that are represented in the book.

3. Invite your toddlers to help you sort the squares by color. You can load them into freight cars or separate them to different "stations" and have your train pick them up along their route.

Tip: This is best for older toddlers who are able to pretend on a smaller scale. Younger toddlers, however, do enjoy having cargo for their trains.

# Train Track
## DRAWING
### Prompt

This has been one of the most popular activities on my blog Bambini Travel, and it is super simple.

**Materials**
Piece of paper
Black marker
Markers and/or crayons
Cups

## What to Do

1. Take a piece of paper (large or small) and draw a simple straight train track along the bottom. I have done this on individual pieces of paper so each toddler works on his own "train" at the art table. I have also done this on a huge piece of paper that stretches the length of the table or a wall, which makes it more of a collaborative experience.

2. Offer different colors of marker or crayons in cups for your toddlers. Depending on their coloring skills, their attempts will look more or less like a train, and that is okay.

3. Encourage them to tell you about their trains. Talk to them about their drawings with comments such as, "Tell me about your drawing," or "What kind of train is running on your tracks?"

# Bike Ride

In some cultures, bike riding is a primary form of transportation. Biking is a wonderful way to exercise and get somewhere. There are several ways to include your toddler in a bike ride. Attachments of various kinds are available to cart your toddler on or behind an adult bike. Most places are to some degree bike-friendly, even if there are not actual bike trails. This is also a fun way to get some exercise while transporting your children. For instance, I frequently bike to a park, let them play, and then bike home.

**BRING**

Make helmets non negotiable.

You may want to bring stuffed animals or books for your toddlers to look at in case they get antsy.

It is also important to make sure they are freshly changed, hydrated, comfortably dressed, and not hungry; otherwise, you will have cranky passengers.

**CONSIDER**

If you are working with a large group of toddlers, consider simply giving a riding demonstration or visiting a bike shop. I worked with a creative teacher in Minneapolis who brought her bike to the center, and the class came outside to investigate it. Many of them had never seen an adult bike or at least had not been invited to touch one, and they were fascinated. Remember that with toddlers the simplest things, such as bikes, are new and interesting.

## Decorate Your TRIKE and Have a PARADE

**Materials**
1 riding toy or push toy per child
Streamers, crepe paper, and ribbon

### What to Do

1. Using streamers and other supplies, decorate your toddlers' trikes.

2. To make this even more fun, invite some friends or another class to decorate trikes as well.

3. When everyone is done, have a parade up and down the block or around an open space.

## RED Light, GREEN Light

Play Red Light, Green Light. This activity works great anywhere in the transportation unit and is a fun gross motor activity for toddlers. You can simply play the traditional way by calling out "Red Light" to mean stop and "Green Light" to mean go.

**Materials**
Red and green construction paper
Contact paper
Scissors (adult use)
Riding toys

### What to Do

1. For toddlers, I also recommend including a visual. Cut a green circle and red circle out of construction paper and laminate them with contact paper for durability.

2. Then, hold up a color and say the word to communicate your message.

3. Let the children play by going on green and stopping on red.

# Visit a Boat

Boats are the vehicles of the water. If you live near an ocean, a lake, or a river, go hunting for boats. Depending on the size of the water, what you find will vary greatly. I have done this with sailboats in a marina, canoes on a rural lake, and bigger ships in a harbor.

**BRING**

Pack a camera, a pen and notepad for questions, and sunscreen.

Life jackets are a must and are usually provided on the boat. Double-check this beforehand.

**CONSIDER**

If you can, arrange to go on a boat to look around, ask questions, or maybe even go for a ride.

Don't be shy of asking friends or class parents whether they know someone with a boat your children can visit.

**NOTICE**

Talk about what your toddlers notice. Introduce some new vocabulary. (It helps to read up on the topic beforehand if you aren't an avid boater.)

More things to try: count the boats you see or count a certain type of boat. Play I Spy to help notice details. Try moving your body like a boat.

# Activities

## BOATS in the Water TUB

Putting some boats in your water table (or even the bathtub) is a fun way to replay your water adventure.

Materials
Sensory table or bathtub
Plastic boats
Water

### What to Do

1. Add some boats to your sensory table or your toddler's next bath to encourage some pretend play.

2. Engage your toddlers in driving the boats around. Use vocabulary, such as *marina, captain, sailboat,* etc., as you play.

## SING "Row, Row, Row Your Boat"

Sing a song and add some movement to encourage your toddlers' development.

Materials
None

### What to Do

1. Sing the song several times to become familiar.

   *Row, row, row your boat*
   *Gently down the stream*
   *Merrily, merrily, merrily, merrily*
   *Life is but a dream*

   *Row, row, row your boat*
   *Gently down the stream*
   *Merrily, merrily, merrily, merrily*
   *Life is but a dream*

2. If you want, you can also add some gross motor movement by sitting on the floor facing each other, holding hands, and "rowing" back and forth as you sing.

# Street Sign Hunt

For a child interested in vehicles, learning the rules of the road is a natural extension. Start by pointing out some signs to your toddler while you drive or asking your class what signs they have seen before. Then, go for a walk to see what street signs are in your area. Look for stop signs, street signs, speed-limit signs, and more. Take photos of what you find.

**BRING** Pack a camera to take photos of signs to discuss with the class later. Seeing the signs again will provide good repetition so that they can begin to learn what each sign means.

**CONSIDER** Scout beforehand a good area with light traffic where you can walk.

## Activities

### DIY SIGN for BLOCK AREA

A new addition to a play area can reinvigorate how your toddlers play there. You can purchase small signs for block play, but it is also easy and inexpensive to make your own.

## What to Do

1. Draw and cut out signs (or print some from on-line) and tape them to paper-towel rolls or blocks you are willing to donate to the project.

2. One of our favorites was a stoplight. Cut black construction paper and wrap it around a paper-towel roll and tape.

3. Then cut small red, yellow, and green circles and attach those to the paper-towel roll as well.

4. Book tape or clear packing tape can help secure the whole thing in place.

5. Add these simple signs to your block area.

## Materials

Photos of basic signs
Book tape or clear packing tape
Construction paper
Paper-towel rolls or blocks

# RED, YELLOW, and GREEN
## Bean Bag Toss

Throwing or tossing is a gross motor skill for toddlers. This is a stoplight-inspired way to practice.

## What to Do

1. Cut and laminate red, yellow, and green circles.

2. Lay them out on the floor or ground outside.

3. Provide a basket with bean bags. (If you don't have bean bags, they are fairly simple to create, but rolled-up socks work pretty well too!)

4. Encourage your children to stand by the basket and toss their bean bags to a color and call out the color name.

## Materials

Red, yellow, and green construction paper
Contact paper
Bean bags
Basket

**Animals are delightful in their diversity.**
Our world is teeming with different animals that move in different ways, are coated in soft furs and colorful feathers, and make an exciting array of noises. Children are often fascinated by animals. Firsthand experiences with animals can only enhance their understanding.

# Animals

# Zoo

Going to the zoo is likely an adventure already on your radar. There are many mixed opinions about zoos, but they are a way for young children to see real animals moving, eating, and playing. Zoos are fun year-round, but if your children are showing an interest in animals or a particular animal, now is the time to plan a trip!

**BRING** Pack something for your toddlers to do at the zoo, such as binoculars to look through, a camera, or notebooks and markers. These items will work if you need to take breaks and slow down a little as you go. You will need the camera to take photos for the "DIY Animal Cards" and the "Move Like an Animal" activities.

**CONSIDER** It is helpful to have a plan. Ask your toddlers what animals they most want to see and start there. Depending on the size of your local zoo, seeing the whole thing might not be possible with little legs, short attention spans, and eating and sleeping schedules. Starting with what they most want to see means no one will leave the zoo devastated.

**NOTICE** The zoo also provides many opportunities to help expand children's vocabulary. Talk about the animals you see and their habitats, and make note of any questions they have.

# Activities

Word cards can be a simple way to expand vocabulary with toddlers.

## DIY ANIMAL Cards

### Materials

Photos of animals
Glue or tape
Card stock or
    construction paper
Marker
Scissors (adult use)
Contact paper or
    laminator

## What to Do

1. Take the photos of animals from your zoo trip or ones you find online and print them out at a 5"x 7" size.

2. Tape or glue them to construction paper or card stock, and trim the paper to frame the photo.

3. On the back or below the picture, write the name of the animal and then laminate your cards (contact paper is a cheap alternative).

4. Place the cards in a basket for your toddler to explore. If they are interested, sit near them and ask what animals they see.

5. Feel free to just have a conversation about it. Do not feel like you have to quiz them on the vocabulary. Toddlers naturally pick up a lot through quiet conversation with an adult.

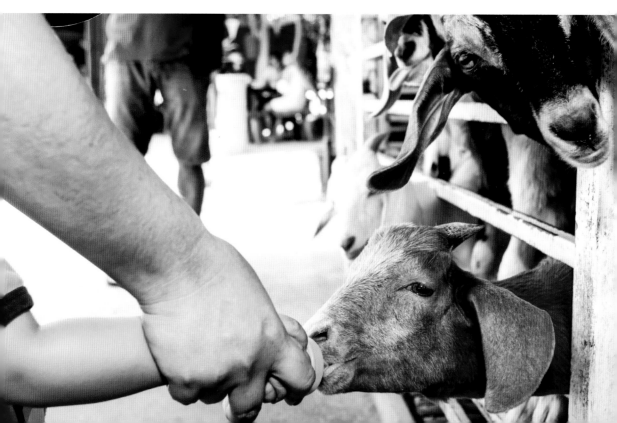

Bring pretend play to your block area once again with some toy animals.

## What to Do

1. Place a basket of animals in your block area.

2. If your children seem interested, offer to make a zoo with them.

3. Then ask, "What does our zoo need?" and let their ideas guide the zoo.

Tip: Younger toddlers may just be interested in playing with the animals on their own. Older toddlers might be interested in making the animals a home or zoo cage or pretending that the blocks are food for their animals. Follow their ideas and expand their play gently as you go.

# Building a BLOCK ZOO

## Materials
Toy animals
Blocks
Basket

# Move Like an ANIMAL

## Materials
Animal cards from the previous activity

Moving like an animal is a fun way to develop gross motor skills.

## What to Do

1. Use your animal cards as prompts. For example: Show your toddlers a picture card of an elephant, have them call out the animal, and then ask, "How does an elephant move?"

2. Move together, slowly stomping your feet and swaying your arm like a trunk.

3. Continue with the other animal cards as long as they sustain interest.

# Pet Store

A pet store is a good, cheap field trip for children interested in pet animals such as dogs, fish, cats, and gerbils. Even if you don't have a pet in your home or classroom, you can still look at the small pets on sale. You should definitely not feel as though you need to buy a pet to make this adventure fun. We've watched new puppies play or fish swimming in tanks without ever bringing one home. The pet store is also a great place to search for things that a pet needs such as food, a leash, and other care items.

**BRING**   Bring the scavenger hunt list included on page 90 to help focus your visit. You may want to pack a list of questions your toddlers have, along with a book about pets.

**CONSIDER**   Make sure to take allergies into account before planning this trip. Often it is just a case of notifying parents so they can prepare their child with allergy medicine in the morning, but getting permission is important.

# Activities

## ANIMAL to HOME Match

Young children like everything to have a home. You can play this game on various scales depending on what materials you have available.

### Materials

Stuffed or toy animals
Photos of animal habitats
  or homes
Basket
Contact paper

### What to Do

1. If you have small toy animals, stuffed animals, or photos of animals, this game will work.

2. Fill a basket with toy animals, next to photos.

3. Print photos of animal homes, and cover each with contact paper. For pets, print homes such as a fish bowl, doghouse, cat bed.

4. Let the children sort animals to different kinds of homes, such as animals that live in a house, animals that live on a farm, and animals that live in the jungle.

5. Invite your children to help you figure out where each animal lives by saying something like, "Can you help me find the dog's house?"

## PET WASH

Good pet owners make sure to wash and groom their pet.

### What to Do

1. This activity is bound to get a little messy, so plan to do it outside or in an area where you don't mind soapy water spilling, such as the bathroom or the kitchen.

2. Lay the materials out like an assembly line: animals, soapy water, clean water, and towels.

3. Invite your toddlers to help you wash their animals.

### Materials

Plastic play animals
Tubs or bowls
Water
Small towels
Soap

# Natural Science Museum

**N**atural science museums offer a range of exhibits and opportunities for learning. What you do depends, at least somewhat, on what your museum has to offer. Look online to find out what your local museum has currently on exhibit. Many times natural science museums have smaller animals such as turtles and fish that your children might enjoy watching. Look at what is available, and start in the exhibit that you think fits your children's interests best. That way, if they really take their time and end up spending all or most of your time there, it is okay.

**BRING** Pack a notebook and pen.

**CONSIDER** If you aren't able to go to a natural science museum because one isn't in your area or you can't transport your group, see if there is something comparable that you can bring into your home, neighborhood, or classroom. For example, some nature programs will visit schools with animals and hands-on activities.

**NOTICE** For younger toddlers, label things that interest them to help expand their vocabulary. Offering simple descriptions and words during outings like this are just one way to play a key role in their language acquisition.

For older toddlers, read abbreviated versions of the sections that interest them. Observe what interests your toddlers the most, which may not be what you expect.

Pay attention to what piques your toddlers' interests and make notes about their questions, words, and comments for the "What We Wonder Book" activity.

# Activities

## Exploring MAGNIFYING Glass Tray

*Artifact* is a big word in the world of natural science. Create an invitation to look more closely at your children's "artifacts."

### What to Do

**Materials**
Magnifying glasses
Trays

1. Go for a nature hunt, and have your children collect things. This can be a more extensive hike in the woods or just a walk around your neighborhood, backyard, or playground.

2. Lay out your "artifacts" or finds on trays with magnifying glasses for your children to look at more closely.

3. Encourage them to explore, and give them some time to feel and look at their finds.

4. Then ask them some questions such as, "What do you notice when you look in your magnifying glass?" or "Tell me about what you can see."

## WHAT WE WONDER Book

Use the notes from your field trip to the natural science museum to make a simple *What We Wonder* book.

### What to Do

1. Use your notes from the museum visit to create a book about their thoughts. To do this, write down your children's questions on one side of the page.

2. On the other side, write down the answers when you find them in the museum, in a book, or through other discoveries. If you can, include photos of the answers.

**Materials**
Construction paper
Marker
Photos (if possible)
Hole punch and rings
Tape or glue

3. Another option that would work better for younger toddlers is to write a "We Saw" book in which you have a photo and a word or two to describe the different things they saw at the museum.

# LOOSE Parts in the BLOCK Area

Loose parts are a way to expand creativity and imagination in the block area.

## What to Do

1. Depending on the age of your toddlers and how much they mouth materials, some loose parts for your block area could include rocks, seashells, sticks, pinecones, leaves, flowers, gems, tree bark, and acorns. Place these in baskets on the floor or a shelf in the block area.

2. Toddlers will likely start by just exploring these materials. They might want to carry them around, put them in bags, etc. These activities are all fine and full of imagination and curiosity.

3. Help them also incorporate the items into block play when you see an opportunity. For example, if they are building a long line of blocks, sit near them and build your own line, but add a pinecone on top of each block. This type of parallel play will lead to mirroring or imitation, and new possibilities will pop into their minds.

## Materials

Blocks
Variety of loose parts
Baskets

---

# Booklist: Animals

This list can help you grow your home or school library with books on all sorts of animals.

*Big Al* by Andrew Clements

*Down by the Station* by Will Hillenbrand

*First Big Book of the Ocean* by Catherine D. Hughes

*Going to the Zoo* by Tom Paxton

*Good Night, Gorilla* by Peggy Rathmann

*My Visit to the Aquarium* by Aliki

*Otis* by Loren Long

*Rumble in the Jungle* by Giles Andreae

*Solomon Crocodile: A Picture Book* by Catherine Rayner

*Spot A Lot Animal Escape* by Steve Smallman

*Ten Little Caterpillars* by Bill Martin Jr.

# Bug Walk

The tiniest creatures are just outside your door. Go on a mini-adventure in your backyard, playground, the forest, a park, or near a pond to find bugs. Get your children excited by reading a book about bugs or making a list of things you think you might see. What bugs can they already name? What did you learn about in the book? Some common ones such as ants, worms, or ladybugs are probably easy to spot most places.

**BRING** If you have a bug-catching kit, magnifying glasses, or other bug-investigating equipment, make sure to take it along.

**CONSIDER** Under logs or large rocks is a great place to look for bugs! Help your toddlers slowly move the object aside and then carefully replace it.

Talk with them about what you are seeing and enhance their vocabulary with new terms from the natural world.

**NOTICE** When you find some bugs, invite your children to look more closely with questions such as, "Where do you think the bug is going?" "What do you see the bug doing?"

## BUG JAR
### Observation

If you don't have fancy store-bought bug catchers, you can make your own with just a few materials.

## What to Do

1. Punch a couple of holes in the lid with your screwdriver, or set the lid on concrete or another flat firm surface and pound a nail through. A knife might also work.

2. Have your children help you find some sticks and leaves to put inside for a bug to crawl on.

3. Together, search for a bug to put in the jar. We found one crawling on a leaf and added it, leaf and all, into our jar.

4. Watch the bug together. Ask what your children see.

5. Listen to their observations. Write down or remember their questions.

6. Don't forget to let the bug go when you are done observing it!

## CLAY
### Bugs

Clay is a fantastic sensory experience for children. (If you don't have clay, playdough will also work for this activity.) Once your children are familiar with the medium (either clay or playdough) you can work with them to expand their explorations.

## What to Do

For a bug unit, one possibility is to create simple bugs with the material. An easy way to do this with older toddlers is to make "earthworms" by rolling pieces of clay. With younger toddlers, pinch the clay into smaller pieces to create ants or another small bug.

## Materials
Clay or playdough

# DAUBERS on BUG Prompt

Bingo daubers are one of the very best art materials for younger toddlers. Unlike crayons, which are sometimes frustrating for toddlers because you have to push down hard to make marks on paper, daubers rub easily and leave brilliant colors. Daubers are fun on their own, but sometimes a drawing prompt is a fun way to extend or expand creativity.

## Materials
Do-A-Dot Art! markers
  or bingo daubers
Construction paper
Markers

## What to Do

1. Using the markers, draw a simple drawing prompt on the paper. For a bug unit, something like a leaf or circles in a row (like a caterpillar) would work.

2. Leave the drawing prompt along with the daubers on the art table as an invitation for your toddlers. Regardless of your prompt, remember that the process is far more important than any product.

# Bird Walk

If your toddlers have noticed birds or show an interest in birds, then a bird walk is in order! Birds are everywhere, so this can take place in your neighborhood, on your playground, or on a nature trail. What you look for and what you see will vary based on your location and the time of year. When we lived in the Midwest, robins were a reliable option. In the South, we saw a huge variety of birds every day including blue jays, cardinals, and even egrets. Here in New York City, we would probably start by hunting for pigeons.

**BRING**  Pack binoculars to help them focus their attention.

**CONSIDER**  Similar to your bug walk, I highly recommend reading a picture book about birds before you go to familiarize your toddlers with what they will be looking for on your walk. Get them excited by asking questions such as, "Can we see if we can find robins or blue jays at the park?"

**NOTICE**  While you walk, take time to stop and listen.
Encourage your children to look up into the trees and look for nests.
Consider asking them to cover their eyes and just listen for sounds of birds.

# Activities

## Fine Motor FEEDING Activity

This is a creative twist on using tweezers with toddlers that incorporates some pretend play.

### What to Do

1. With this activity your toddlers will be pretending their eye dropper, tweezers, and deep scoop tongs are bird mouths. Set out the eye dropper, tweezers, and tongs.

2. In a small bowl place red dyed water. In the other two bowls, place brown pieces of string and small plastic fish. These will be the "food."

3. Invite your children to pretend to be a hummingbird (eye dropper and red dyed water), robin (tweezers and "earth-worms"), and a seagull (tongs and plastic fish) and use the fine motor tool to pretend to eat the "food."

4. Having pictures of these animals available can help children connect the birds to their play.

5. For younger toddlers, pick one type of fine motor skill/bird to practice per day.

### Materials

Eye dropper
Tweezers
Deep scoop tongs
3 small bowls
Red food coloring
Brown pieces of string
Small plastic fish or something similar
Water
Photos of a humming-bird, a seagull, and robin (optional)

## Cardboard WINGS

Pretend to be a bird by creating simple cardboard wings.

### What to Do

1. Use the natural bend in the box to be the fold in your wings.

2. Consider having your toddler help decorate the cardboard with paints, glitter, or washi tape before you start crafting them into wings.

### Materials

Boxes or pieces of cardboard
Scissors (adult use)
Hole punch
String, ribbon, or elastic
Paints, glitter, washi tape, etc.

3. Cut a wing shape on both sides, and then attach string or ribbon to make them wearable.

4. A hole punch and string, ribbon, or elastic looped through will make holds for arms or hands.

5. For classroom use, you will want to make at least four to five pairs of wings.

# Listening for BIRDS in the BACKYARD

In some ways this is another adventure but it will take place right in your backyard or out on the playground. This activity focuses on the sounds birds make.

## What to Do

### Materials

Large paper
Photos of common
   birds
Markers
Glue or tape

1. First, prepare a chart. Print some photos of birds that are common in your area. For instance, we had a robin, blue jay, sparrow, and cardinal on our chart. Here in New York City, I would definitely put pigeon on my list. If you can't print them, draw them the best you can.

2. Write both the bird names and their calls on the chart. You can find recordings of bird calls on the internet. Write your best phonetic estimate of what the bird sounds like.

3. Now you are ready to look and listen. Take your chart outside or on your hike, along with a marker or pen to cross off the birds you hear.

4. Find somewhere to sit or stand and look around. Encourage your children to look up toward the trees for movement.

5. Spend some time covering your eyes to focus on listening.

6. Encourage them to describe what they are seeing/hearing and explain their conclusions. For example: "Why does that look like a cardinal to you?" Mark off the birds you see and hear on your chart.

# Aquarium

For a child who loves fish or water, the aquarium is an ideal field trip. The best aquariums bring underwater worlds to life on the biggest stage with huge tanks full of different aquatic creatures.

A lot of aquariums are quite large and you shouldn't feel as if you need to see every inch of it on your trip. Focus on the parts that interest your children most. For larger aquariums, start where you are most excited to visit. You won't feel anxious about fitting it in and it will be less crowded earlier in the day.

**CONSIDER** For anyone unable to go to an aquarium, consider other ways you might be able to go to see fish or bring fish into your classroom. Some aquariums welcome school visits. You could also make an additional trip to a pet store or visit another classroom that has a big fish tank.

At one of my centers in Minnesota, our lobby had a huge fish tank that spanned the length of our entrance. It was not the same as an aquarium, but our young toddlers still loved to walk down there and watch the fish.

**NOTICE** Invite your children to look closely at the tanks by asking questions such as, "Which fish is your favorite?" and "What are the fish doing in the tank?" Take your time and follow your children's lead.

# Rainbow Fish
# CONTACT
## Paper Collage

This activity is based on the book *The Rainbow Fish* by Marcus Pfister.

## Materials

*The Rainbow Fish*
  by Marcus Pfister
Contact paper
Light table (optional)
Permanent marker
Painter's tape
Aluminum foil
Translucent binder dividers
Tissue paper
Basket or container

## What to Do

1. Read *The Rainbow Fish* by Marcus Pfister a couple of times with your toddlers first.

2. To prepare this activity, pull out a sheet of contact paper cut to cover the light table or a low window. Before you reveal the sticky side, draw some fish outlines on the nonsticky side with a marker. My talents do not lie in drawing, but my basic shapes worked fine. Do not stress about your abilities.

3. Reveal the sticky side and tape it, sticky side out, onto the light table or window with painter's tape.

4. Tear or cut aluminum foil, tissue paper, and binder dividers (my light table material of choice for collages) into varying sizes and shapes.

5. Put these in a basket or container at the table. I also placed the book on the table for reference.

6. During playtime, invite your toddlers to help you make some rainbow fish at the light table, or even better, allow them to discover it on their own and then explain your thought if needed.

7. Try not to worry about the paper all ending up on the fish. We focused our attention on using fine motor skills to put the colors where we wanted and using cognitive and language skills to practice recognizing and describing the colors we were using. Between the book and the "fish" on the table, my toddlers figured it out pretty quickly. They were especially excited to add the foil to make the fish shiny.

8. When the collage is complete, you can stick it to the wall or window.

## Ordering FISH by Size

Ordering is a basic math skill. This activity helps children practice putting things in order by size.

### What to Do

1. Make the fish by drawing a simple fish shape on construction paper in three different sizes—small, medium, and large. Make several fish of each size.

2. Use contact paper or a laminator to make them more durable for your toddlers.

3. Place the fish in a basket in your play area.

4. When your toddlers are interested, encourage them to explore the fish first. They might want to "swim" them around or explore them in other ways.

### Materials

Construction paper
Scissors
Contact paper
  (or a laminator)
Basket

5. Then ask if they would like to help you put them in order. Ask them to find the big fish, then the middle fish, then the smallest fish.

6. Place them in order, and then see if they want to do it again.

7. Older toddlers might also enjoy making patterns with the fish. Start with the most basic pattern, ABAB. For example, line up a big fish, a small fish, and then a big fish and ask your toddlers what they think comes next.

## Pet Store Scavenger Hunt

Search for pet gear, food, and other supplies with this pet store scavenger list. Add any more items you think the children would enjoy searching for in the store.

Leash

Bird

Fish

Animal toy

Dog food

Reptile

Cat or dog food bowl

Grooming supplies

Animal bed

# Pond Walk

**D**o you have a pond or river near your home or school? They are fun places to get outside and explore at your toddlers' pace. If you are lucky, you will also spot some animals.

Make sure to explain your expectations beforehand to your toddlers. I insisted that toddlers stay together in our small groups. Carefully monitoring children near water is always essential. Giving them things to look for and keeping them engaged with conversation helped to keep us naturally together.

**BRING** Wear boots. Ponds tend to be muddy.

Bring some supplies for gathering findings or looking more closely at your environment, such as bug jars, binoculars, or magnifying glasses. Don't feel like you need to take all of these things each time, but take something to engage your toddlers in exploration.

**NOTICE** Explore the area. Look under rocks and logs. Draw attention to any wildlife you spot. See what interests your toddler and do more of that.

--- ## Activities ---

### FLOATS or SINKS Experiment

This early experiment is perfect for toddlers. Tip: Check before you begin to make sure you have some sinking items and floating items, because you might be surprised by what sinks and what floats.

## What to Do

Note: Younger toddlers might not have interest in the more official parts of the experiment. For these toddlers, simply present them with a collection of items and use the words *sink* and *float* in your conversations and descriptions of their play.

1. Start by making a simple chart with a column for items, a column labeled *sink* and a column labeled *float*.

2. List each item to test in the first column.

3. Before you put the items in your water tub, ask your toddlers to make a hypothesis about whether it will sink or float.

4. Then have them help you X the column for where it fits.

Contact paper is a fabulous material to use for making collages with toddlers.

# FEATHER
## Contact Paper
# COLLAGE

## What to Do

1. Cut a large piece of contact paper and tape it face side up to the table or the wall.

2. Place a basket of feathers nearby for your toddlers to explore. (Fake ones can easily be ordered online or found at a craft store.) The great thing about contact-paper collages is that your toddlers can stick feathers on and pull them off over and over again. It plays perfectly into their need to repeat behaviors.

3. Try leaving this up for a few days in a row so they can come and go from the activity.

# Farm

Farm animals are often some of the first animal sounds that a toddler learns. If your toddlers enjoy mooing and clucking, take them to see the real thing! Many pick-your-own farms have a petting zoo. Another option for city folk is to visit the farm area at a zoo.

**BRING** Pack a camera and hand sanitizer (if it is a petting zoo).

**CONSIDER** If you can't go to a farm, can a farm come to you? The first center I worked at had a petting zoo come to our playground each summer. The children got to pet llamas and feed goats right behind our school for a morning.

**NOTICE** Some things to do at the farm could include looking for your favorite animal, listening to the sounds that the real animals make and trying to imitate them, and taking photos of the animals.

Pay attention to details such as where the animals are living or what they are eating.

# Activities

## BUILDING Block FARMS

Adding farm animals to your block area is a simple idea that can dramatically alter your toddlers' block play.

### What to Do

1. Add toy farm animals to the block area.

2. Give your toddlers a few days and see how they play with the animals. Do they include them at all in their block play? How? If they haven't incorporated them at all after a few days, consider leaving them an invitation.

3. Create an invitation by making a simple block creation with an animal. For example, four blocks can make a fenced pen and add a cow in the middle.

### Materials
Play farm animals
Blocks

4. Remember your toddlers' block-playing skills when you create this invitation. You want to be scaffolding their play to the next level, not creating something they are not capable of making on their own and thus intimidating them and taking over their play.

## PIGSTY Sensory Bin

Create a farm-themed sensory bin for your toddlers to explore.

### What to Do

1. Fill a sensory table or tub with mud (or if you are looking for something less messy, shredded brown construction paper).

2. Add some toy pigs, shovels, and small bowls.

3. Encourage your toddlers to stomp, dig, scoop, and pretend with the pigs.

### Materials
Sensory table or tub
Mud or shredded brown
   construction paper
Toy pigs
Shovels
Small bowls

# Hike

**V**isit a trail in a state or national park and go for a hike with your toddlers. The age of children in your group will dictate a lot about your hike. Follow your children's lead. As they get older, hikes will become more and more focused if you begin when they are young. For now, embrace a few moments to look around and notice something more carefully, and let the rest be a free exploration.

**BRING**    Pack binoculars to help you spot animals and a bag for collecting things (make sure that collecting things is allowed where you are hiking).

**CONSIDER**    Hiking can be challenging for children in wheelchairs, those who have difficulty walking, and those with sensory processing disorders. Consider their needs when planning your location, duration, and expectations.

**NOTICE**    Since your toddlers will likely be rather loud in the forest, take a few "listening breaks" to try to hear animals around you. Stop together, listen, and ask questions such as, "What can you hear?" Invite your children to look up in the trees and down on the trail to see what they can find.

# PLAYDOUGH and STICKS

Playdough is a great creative material, but it is also excellent for developing fine motor skills. Change up your toddlers' playdough explorations by adding some natural loose parts.

## Materials

Loose parts (sticks, rocks, leaves, etc.)
Playdough or clay

## What to Do

1. Present the loose parts you found alongside a ball of playdough for each toddler.

2. What can they do with the new materials? Poke? Pound? Make an impression in the dough? What might animals do with these sticks?

# HIKE Mystery Texture BAG

Texture bags are a fun way to isolate the sense of touch. It is a great sensory experience but also helps to develop vocabulary for describing textures.

## What to Do

1. Place natural items in pairs inside a cloth bag.

2. After you place the pairs inside, invite your toddlers to play a game.

3. Have them feel inside the bag. They should use only their sense of touch.

4. Have them pull out one item and then, using their sense of touch, try to find the match.

## Materials

Cloth bag (paper bags work in a pinch)
Pairs of natural items (2 rocks, 2 sticks, 2 leaves, 2 pebbles, etc.)

# BEAR HUNT
## Backyard Pretend
## PLAY

### Materials
*We're Going on a Bear Hunt* picture book

To enjoy this pretend play, you will need to read or at least tell the story of *We're Going on a Bear Hunt*. I highly recommend the version written by Michael Rosen and illustrated by Helen Oxenbury.

## What to Do

1. Read the story several times to familiarize yourself and your toddlers with the story.

2. Then head into the backyard or a trail and reenact the story. It may be helpful to take the story along with you.

3. Get into the storytelling. Be dramatic with your voice and body to engage your children in the story.

## — Spotlight on Gross Motor Development —

In today's society of tablets and smartphones, it is sometimes hard to determine where gross motor skills fit in. Gross motor skills, however, continue to be important for learning to navigate our world and for fostering the habit of movement. Children who are active when young are more likely to stay active and fit into adulthood.

When I worked in child care, an hour outdoors daily both in the morning and in the afternoon was mandatory. The positives of being outside are plentiful, but the opportunity for gross motor movement is an important aspect of this time.

Some simple ways to foster gross motor development:

• Carve out daily time in your schedule to move.

• Try fitting a daily yoga session into your schedule, perhaps in the morning or before naptime. We love the *ABCs of Yoga for Kids* cards for inspiration.

• Model gross motor activity. Whether you take time every week to go to the gym or take a walk with your children, model the importance of finding time to move.

• Make it fun. Find a gross motor activity that is enjoyable for your children, and build on that.

• Keep it simple. An easy running game is often all toddlers need to get excited about moving. "Show me how fast you can run around that tree and back to me!" is all you need.

# Visit a Pet

This field trip requires you to know someone with a pet. If you have one of your own, consider asking someone with a different sort of a pet if you can visit. Regardless, arrange for your toddlers to visit some kind of pet. Use your knowledge of your toddlers to determine what kind of pet is best for them to visit. If you work with toddlers in a classroom, ask someone to bring a pet to visit or visit another class's pet. A variety of pets will work for this activity including fish, guinea pigs, or turtles. I have done this activity with a wide range of animals. The important thing to remember is to prepare your toddlers.

We had a dog come to visit our school. This was an exceptionally gentle dog trained to visit children in hospitals. Before our visit, we talked to our toddlers about using quiet voices, only touching the dog's back, and that they could help the dog's owner, one at a time, by gently brushing the dog's fur.

**BRING** Consider packing a treat or snack for the pet (check with the owner beforehand!).

**CONSIDER** Talk to the pet owner beforehand to ensure that everyone has a smooth and happy visit. Ask whether it will be okay to feed or groom the pet.

If you are working in a classroom, it is also important to get parental permission for their child to interact with a new animal and to make sure you don't have any pet allergies to keep in mind when choosing which animal to visit.

**NOTICE** Prepare your children ahead of time, and discuss what the pet might do, what they can do to interact with the pet and what they should not do.

## Activities

# MAKE a LEASH
## for Your
# STUFFED ANIMAL

Toddlers love pushing and pulling things. This activity provides them an additional opportunity for pulling something.

## What to Do

1. Simply tie a ribbon around the neck or middle of a stuffed animal. I used a darling collection of animals from an infant floor mat that went out of use when our little guys started moving. Most stuffed animals would work, although ones with four legs balance a little better.

2. Model taking the animal for a walk.

3. Keep the animals with leashes on the shelf for the children to explore.

Safety note: The free end of the leash should be no longer than 8 inches. Always supervise the children closely when they are playing with the leashes.

### Materials
Construction paper
Scissors
Markers
Hole punch
Ribbon
Stuffed animals

Pretend play requires some props. Invite your toddlers to make a water and/or food bowl for their "pets" (stuffed animals).

# Decorate a
# WATER and
# FOOD BOWL
## for Your Pet

## What to Do

1. Invite your toddlers to decorate their pet bowls with stickers.

2. Then, work together to add "food" to the bowl, such as crumpled construction paper or something similar.

3. Add this to your play space for your toddlers to use with their stuffed animal "pets."

### Materials
Plastic or paper bowls
Stickers
Stuffed animals
Construction paper

# Art
## Museum

**M**useums are beautiful and inspiring, even for little ones if you approach your visit with children in mind. If your toddlers love to create art, the art museum is a natural field trip. For this unit, focus on finding animals in the artwork.

During the visit, pick one exhibit or a few paintings to focus on to avoid overwhelming your little ones. It is helpful to pick out these pieces before you head to the museum with your children. Often you can find the collections online.

**BRING** Pack a camera, drawing paper, and pencils.

**CONSIDER** Visit early in the day or on a weekday when it isn't as crowded. Talk to your children beforehand about what to expect and expectations for behavior. Read books about art and art museums. You can also get excited by painting or creating together.

Think creatively if you can't visit an art museum. Can you create one in your room or in a hallway of your school? Can you visit another classroom's art display? Can you do a virtual tour of an art museum online?

**NOTICE** Have your children pick a favorite piece. Have them tell you about it. What is happening? What do they like about it? How do they think it was made?

Take a picture (if allowed) of it to investigate further at home and/or draw a sketch of it in the museum.

# BIG ART

There is something about an immense canvas that is exciting. While it would be fun for just one child to attack a huge piece of paper, I also love the collaborative aspect that is added when children work side by side on a huge work of art.

## What to Do

1. Make space on a large wall where the children can create.

2. Cover the wall in white paper, place cups with markers on the floor, and plan to leave it up for a few days so they can come and go as they want to work on their picture during playtime.

## Materials
Lots of white paper
Cups
Markers
Tape

Simple rule: The markers need to stay by the paper. It is helpful to know that while this rule is simple to state, learning it often takes lots of patient reminders. Once toddlers learn to respect the classroom and keep markers in your designated art area, however, you have so many more options, so hang in there and keep calmly reminding them and walking their markers back to the art space as needed. It is possible to teach even young toddlers to keep markers in a specific area with this gentle guidance.

# CREATE an Art Museum WALK

Create a miniature art museum of your toddlers' work, then take a tour to view the art.

## What to Do

1. Hang the children's art pieces on a wall in an attractive manner. You might want to use black paper to frame your children's art or use actual frames with the glass removed.

2. Also, write a label for each piece of artwork with the medium used (markers, tempera paint, etc.), the toddler's name, and a title if he wishes to add one.

3. For a little extra fun, consider having your toddlers give someone a tour of their art museum.

## Materials
Various artworks
Large black paper
Labels
Marker or pen

# FRAME
## Drawing Prompt

Sometimes all someone needs to reignite her interest or change her approach is a little prompt. Invite your toddlers to be museum artists by offering them a frame prompt.

## What to Do

1. Draw a simple frame on the paper, leaving a nice large drawing space in the middle.

2. Make sure to use the word *frame* when you invite them to come draw. For example, ask, "Would you like to be an artist and create something in this frame?" This is one of my favorite art prompts.

3. When they are done, display the art on a wall like at a museum.

### Materials
Large piece of paper
Permanent marker
Drawing materials
Tape

# Butterfly Exhibit

**B**utterfly gardens exist in many places. They are often located within museums or gardens. Sometimes they are permanent year-round exhibits, while others visit for a season each year. Search in your area to find one near you. I personally love visiting butterfly gardens. I know they freak some people out, but I think butterflies are beautiful and fascinating in their diversity.

The first time our twins saw a real butterfly was at a butterfly exhibit, and they were entranced. Our son waited with impressive patience and persistence for a butterfly to land on his finger, and it was easily the highlight of the museum trip for him.

**BRING** Pack a camera to take photos of the butterflies.

**CONSIDER** If you aren't able to visit a butterfly garden, hopefully there is somewhere else nearby where you are likely to observe a butterfly. I worked at one center that planted a butterfly garden. Another center had a park with a garden nearby that we could walk our toddlers to and look at flowers and butterflies.

**NOTICE** Know your children. If a child is sensitive to touch, the idea of butterflies flying around his head and potentially landing on him might be scary.

Prepare your children. Let them know what they will be seeing. Talk about the butterflies beforehand.

Stress the importance of being gentle and quiet. Butterflies are extremely fragile and easy to startle.

To get them to land, find a spot near some butterflies where you can sit. Encourage the children to be quiet and to move slowly.

Take pictures so you can remember your favorites and look up more about them later.

# Activities

## Symmetry PAINTING

Butterflies are known for many things, including their natural symmetry. Explore this concept further by creating symmetrical paintings.

### Materials
Construction paper
Paint
Paintbrush

### What to Do

1. Fold pieces of construction paper in half.

2. Have your toddlers paint whatever they want on one half of the paper.

3. When they are done, help them fold over the other half of the paper on top of their painting.

4. Encourage them to press the two sides together.

5. Then unfold the paper, and voilá! a mirror image.

## WIRE and BEADS Butterflies

Stringing beads onto wire requires fine motor control and coordination.

### Materials
Beads
Wire
Wire cutters (adult use)

### What to Do

Tip: Choose a bead size depending on the age of your children and the level of their fine motor skills. The smaller the bead, the more difficult it is to manipulate.

1. Gather wire, beads, and wire cutters. (All materials can be ordered online or found at your local craft store.)

2. Cut the wire to 12-inch lengths. Fold one end of each wire into a small loop to keep the beads from falling off.

3. Invite your toddlers to string beads onto the wire to make a butterfly. Children will need to be approximately two years old to successfully string beads onto wire. Make it one long continuous line of beads.

4. When a child is done, manipulate the string of beads into a butterfly shape, and hang it somewhere so it can "fly" above you.

5. Older toddlers might want to make the butterfly shape themselves. Embrace their desire for independence and accept whatever they give you labeled as a butterfly. Remember that it is the process that matters, not the product.

With an appetizing tempter, encourage some butterflies to come to your garden.

# SUGAR SWEET Nectar for BUTTERFLIES

## What to Do

1. Start by punching a ¼-inch hole in the lid of the jar with your nail and hammer.

2. Prepare the nectar (4 parts water to 1 part sugar, boiled and cooled).

3. Invite your toddlers to decorate the outside of the jar with either the acrylic paint or flower stickers. If you are worried about your toddlers eating the paint, use the stickers.) Remember that butterflies like bright colors.

4. When your toddlers are done with the outside and the paint has dried (if applicable), screw the lid firmly onto the jar.

5. Fill the hole you created in the lid of the jar with a piece of cotton soaked with the nectar.

### Materials
Jars with lids
Cotton
Water
Sugar
Twine or string
Waterproof paint or
    stickers
Hammer and small nail
    (for adult use only)

6. Tie a loop of twine around the lid of the jar, and hang it in your garden.

7. If you want to keep your butterfly feeder long term, you will need to clean it periodically with hot water and bleach to avoid mold growing in the jar.

# State Fair

I f your toddlers enjoy farm animals, a state or county fair is a fun place to meet them up close. You can see a variety of farm animals, and some fairs even have a place where you can pet some of the animals.

Our favorite place to visit is always the barns. There, we get to see a variety of farm animals, up close. We might even meet a friendly farmer or two who is willing to answer your toddlers' questions about pigs or cows.

**BRING**    Pack hand sanitizer and a camera.

**CONSIDER**    Check the schedule beforehand to see if you can plan to attend when there are some animal events.

**NOTICE**    If your children are feeling brave, they also might have an opportunity to ask a farmer questions about the animals.

Prepare by reading some books about farm animals and putting out some toy animals for your toddlers to play with before your trip.

## Activities

### Playdough and ANIMALS

Playdough is another fun material that I like to try different things with to expand and adapt play.

### What to Do

1. Place the playdough and toy farm animals in an attractive manner on a table for your toddlers to explore. If you have some plastic fences or other barn props that are washable, consider including those.

2. Encourage your toddlers to play however they wish, but if they are looking for some direction, suggest that they flatten out the playdough first.

3. Then you could model for them how a cow might walk across the playdough or pretend to eat it as "grass." See where their imaginations go from there.

## Materials
Green playdough
Toy farm animals
Plastic toy farm props
(optional)

# ANIMALS in a BARN

Get ready to build a barn with your child.

## What to Do

1. Tell your toddlers that you are animals and you need a barn. Ask them if they will help you build a barn to live in.

2. Hang some blankets or sheets over a table, a shelf, or some couches and chairs.

3. Once the fort/barn is built, engage in pretend play with your toddlers. Pretend you are a farm animal and crawl around. Make mooing sounds.

4. Or, if you would rather, gather some stuffed animals that resemble farm animals and act out what they might do in the barn.

## Materials
Blankets or sheets
Chairs, tables, or shelves
Stuffed animals or
   animal costumes
   (both optional)

Whether you want to pretend to be animals or you would like to walk some barn animal stuffed friends, gather everyone for an animal show.

# Have an ANIMAL Show

## What to Do

1. If you are pretending to be the animals, a little face paint and a ribbon tail could go a long way to completing the illusion for a concrete thinker like a toddler.

2. March all the animals around, and then give out ribbons for silly prizes such as craziest hair or best animal sound.

## Materials
Face paint (optional)
Animal costumes
Stuffed animals

**Animals are just one small part of what makes our planet so fascinating.**
Children observe everything, and their curiosity about weather, plant life, and the textures and sights around them is boundless. Often just being in nature heightens our awareness of the world and draws us into the mysteries that are everywhere. Head outside with the children to enjoy and explore everything our world has to offer.

# Our World

# Rainy Day Walk

**M**y instinct on a rainy day is to curl up on the couch with a good book, but children are often intrigued by the rain. They also love any excuse to don their rain gear. Find a warm rainy day and head out for a rainy-day walk.

**BRING** Make sure to dress for the rain. Rain boots, raincoats, and a hat or umbrella are highly recommended.

**NOTICE** Hunt for puddles. See if you can spot worms. Try to catch rain on your tongues.

## Activities

### Materials
Powdered drink-mix packets
Bowls
Paper
Paintbrushes
A rainy day

### RAIN Painting

This is such a fun (and delicious-smelling) activity for a rainy day.

### What to Do

1. Have your toddlers help you pour the drink-mix powder into a bowl, one flavor per bowl.

2. Carefully carry your bowls outside and set them down where the rain can fall into the bowls. The rainwater will mix with the drink mix and create watercolors.

3. Bring the bowls back inside to the table. Paint on your paper and enjoy the fun scents.

Practice simple measuring skills with this activity.

## What to Do

1. Place the jars out in the rain. If possible, place them where your children can see them from inside.

2. When the rain stops, bring your cups inside and measure how much water you have. A simple liquid measuring cup would work for this.

3. Extension idea: If there is a lot of rain in the forecast, repeat this activity for several days to see which day it rains the most!

# Collect RAIN and MEASURE

### Materials
2 clean jars
Liquid measuring cup

# MAKE up a RAIN DANCE

Stuck inside for days due to rain? Let's dance!

## What to Do

### Materials
Music

Raining for days? Do a backward rain dance to make the rain go away! Or just dance like a raindrop—what would that look like? How about a thunderstorm; how do thunderclouds dance? Turn on some music and have fun.

# Puddle Walk

**P**uddle walks are a blast. Be prepared to get soaked and embrace it. Boots are a must (for grown-ups too!). Plan to head out after a heavy rain. Search for puddles and then stomp, jump, and splash. This is fantastic fun and a great gross motor exercise. Never has there been a better reason to jump.

Have towels and dry clothing ready to change into after the walk.

**CONSIDER** Scout out puddles beforehand so you avoid disappointment.

## Activities

### Watercolor PAINT

Make some watercolor paintings in celebration of the watery weather outside.

#### What to Do

Tip: If your toddlers haven't done watercolor painting before, you need to do some instruction the first time.

1. To teach them the basic process, help them remember the steps by repeating the words: *Water. Paint. Paper.*

2. Dip your brush in the water, put your brush in the paint, and then move it to the paper.

3. Then move your brush back to the water when you want to choose a different color.

### Materials
Watercolor paints
Paintbrushes
Watercolor paper (works so much better than other paper)

# BLOCK
## Area PUDDLES

This is one of the sillier things I have added to a block area, but it was also a lot of fun.

## Materials

Aluminum foil
Blue construction paper
Tape
1 Toy animal or person

## What to Do

1. Use some foil and blue construction paper to create some simple puddles in your block area. Either would work, but I like them best together, with the foil taped onto the blue construction paper.

2. Add some animals or toy people that can pretend to stomp in the puddles. It is likely that your children won't know what the puddles are at first, so if they ask, explain that they are puddles like the ones you saw on your puddle walk.

3. Pull an animal or person out and model for the children how to jump and splash in a puddle. Younger toddlers will likely want to jump on the puddles themselves. Adjust your mindset to the fact that the puddles will probably tear, and that is okay.

## Floating BOATS Puddle

Have a truly awesome puddle? This is a fun way to play in one.

## What to Do

1. Find some plastic boats or look online for some DIY instructions, and head outside.

2. Pretend that the puddle is a lake or a river, and send those boats on a ride.

## Materials

Plastic boats
A good puddle

# Garden
# Center

It might be easier to gather the gardening supplies at the garden center on your own, but I encourage you to resist the urge. With your toddlers, make a list of what you need. Draw pictures of each item next to the word to enable them to help and to start to draw the connection between words and meaning. This is the sort of learning through adventure that gives children a meaningful context for a concept.

**CONSIDER** Focus only on what you need for this project. It is tempting to take care of other errands, but keeping it focused helps your children stay involved and draw a connection between making the list, buying the supplies, and planting.

The younger your toddlers are, the shorter you want this list to be so that they will stay focused on the task.

**NOTICE** At the garden center, offer your children choices where you can. "This type of seed or this one?" "Do you want to plant purple flowers or red ones?" As you shop, refer back to the list often to demonstrate the value of reading and list making. If they are interested, help them read the labels on the items you are buying.

## Activities

## FLOWER
### Color Sorting

This activity combines real materials and hands-on math.

### What to Do

1. Gather some flowers or petals, either from the garden center or your garden. Make sure you have a variety of colors for this activity.

2. Place all of the flowers or petals in a basket, and place the markers nearby if you are using them.

3. When your children are interested, spread out the color markers and then invite your children to sort by color. You can either give them this direction orally or demonstrate the activity by moving a couple of the flowers to their matching color.

Planting with toddlers is a great hands-on opportunity to learn about the planting process.

# Planting SEEDS

## What to Do

Tip: It is helpful to prepare all of the materials ahead of time so that each child has a prepared planting station.

1. Lay newspaper or any large paper to cover the surface you are using, unless you are doing the activity outside.

2. Have a small pot for each type of plant you plan to grow.

3. Prepare a larger pot or bowl full of dirt and a scoop—measuring scoops work well for us.

4. Have a packet of seeds handy but unopened.

5. Then, with everything prepared, invite your children to plant, or if they helped you pick out the supplies earlier, remind them of your plan to plant together.

6. Have them scoop dirt into their pots.

7. Demonstrate how to poke a hole with a finger for the seeds and then invite them to try. Put seeds in the holes—this does not need to be perfect, but encourage them to spread the seeds out in the pot.

8. Scoop more dirt to cover up the seeds.

9. Have them help you fill up a watering can or a cup at the sink if they can reach. Then carefully carry it back and water the seeds.

10. Talk about how it will be their job to water the seeds a couple of times a week.

11. Together, find a sunny place to put your pots.

# Garden Center DRAMATIC Play

Pretend play or dramatic play is an excellent way for children to deepen their understanding of and practice roles or ideas they have witnessed in life.

## What to Do

1. Wrap the empty container with construction paper. Write the word *dirt* on the container.

2. Tear up and ball pieces of the brown construction paper. This will be the dirt. Place it in the container.

3. Cover the seed packets with contact paper, for durability.

4. Set out the pots, container of dirt, scoops, and seed packets on a tray for the children to explore.

5. Model planting the seeds for your toddlers.

### Materials
Tray
Empty seed packets
Small pots
Measuring scoops
Empty container
Brown construction paper
Contact paper
Marker

---

# Booklist: Our World

The titles below, from *The Gruffalo* to *The Gigantic Turnip*, can help children learn and wonder about what makes up the world we live in.

*10 Things I Can Do to Help My World* by Melanie Walsh

*All the Water in the World* by George Ella Lyon and Katherine Tillotson

*Blueberries for Sal* by Robert McCloskey

*Finding Wild* by Megan Wagner Lloyd

*The Gigantic Turnip* by Aleksei Tolstoy

*The Gruffalo* by Julia Donaldson

*Inside Outside* by Lizi Boyd

*Lola Plants a Garden* by Anna McQuinn

*Night Animals* by Gianna Marino

*Tap Tap Boom Boom* by Elizabeth Bluemle

*Thunderstorm* by Arthur Geisert

*We're Going on a Leaf Hunt* by Steve Metzger

# Nature Center

Nature centers are delightful spots, often located within a community. They have a range of services for families and children that often include hiking trails, small animals and other animal artifacts, and family programming. Visit your nature center's website to see what services they offer and what would work best for you and your toddlers.

**BRING**

Pack bags for collecting the little things children find, such as rocks, leaves, and sticks.

It is also helpful to bring binoculars or cameras, both of which help toddlers slow down a little and pause to look more at the area around them.

**CONSIDER**

When you are planning a hike, make sure to consider elevation, weather, and your children's age when you are choosing a hiking trail. Most toddlers can walk a maximum of one mile on relatively flat ground.

If hills are inevitable, try very hard to avoid having them at the end of your hike when the children's legs are tired.

You also want to dress for the weather and plan for a shorter time frame if it is colder or wet, even if you are wearing appropriate clothes.

# Crayon TEXTURE Drawings

Did you gather any leaves or other flat items on your walk? Then this is perfect for your toddlers.

## What to Do

1. Have your toddlers help lay a leaf on the tabletop and place a piece of paper on top. Secure the paper's corners with masking tape so it doesn't slide around.

2. Rub the long side of the crayon across the entire object, creating a print.

### Materials

Leaves
Copy paper
Crayons (with wrapping removed)
Masking tape
Magnifying glasses (optional)

3. Another option is to head outside. Find a tree or some other textured surface and do a rubbing in the field.

4. What do you notice when you look carefully at the rubbing? Grab a magnifying glass and look even closer.

# Reenact the GRUFFALO

Have you read *The Gruffalo* by Julia Donaldson? It is a hilarious book about a mouse who goes for a walk in the woods. Along his way he frightens away the hungry animals he meets with his tale of a Gruffalo. This works until he actually meets the Gruffalo. Read this delightful story with the children.

## What to Do

1. Act out the story, pretending to be the various animals. Use the stuffed animals as the characters for the story. If you are doing this with a group of toddlers, you could assign a character to a toddler or two or three toddlers. It is, however, helpful if they can all have something to hold.

### Materials

Various stuffed or other toy animals
*The Gruffalo* by Julia Donaldson

2. It is okay, especially with older toddlers, to retell the story using animals different from those actually in the story. They will be able to understand the substitutions if you explain that you are making your own version. For instance, "In our version, the mouse is this teddy bear."

3. How much you retell the story versus having your toddlers retell the story depends on three things: their age, how often you have already done a retelling activity, and how familiar they are with this story. The youngest toddlers will just be entertained to watch you retell the story (as long as you do it with plenty of expression); whereas, the oldest toddlers can likely tell most of the story with the book for a prompt.

# NATURE
## Photography

Children love an opportunity to try their hand at anything they see grown-ups do. Cameras are a relatively simple tool that a toddler can learn to use with a little guidance.

### Materials
1 camera per toddler

## What to Do

1. Take the children outside somewhere: your neighborhood, a garden, the forest.

2. Ask them if they would like to take a picture, when you see them notice something in particular.

3. Patiently teach them how to hold the camera, where to look, and where to push to take the picture; then step back. Like anything else, they will need to explore and make some mistakes before they master this new skill.

4. If they are interested, when you get home or back to the classroom, help them download the images and pick a couple of favorites to print. Continue to offer this activity in different locations over time to encourage mastery.

Tip: Due to the fine motor skills involved in holding a camera and taking a picture, I recommend this more for older toddlers. Because you need one camera per child and due to the one-on-one time needed to teach this skill, this is best for small groups of toddlers at a time.

# State Park

Many people live within a short drive of a state or national park. This is awesome news because parks are a source of natural beauty, history, and more. Find one that is nearby and plan a visit. Check their website first for information about cost, parking, activities available, etc.

I recommend stopping at the park ranger's office for a map and some tips on the most toddler-friendly trails. Then, go for a hike. Explore whatever the park has to offer: the view, the climb, the water, or whatever else there is to see.

**BRING** Make sure to pack water, binoculars or cameras (one per child if possible), snacks, bug spray, and sunscreen.

**CONSIDER** For classrooms with toddlers who likely cannot ride the bus, this may be more difficult to access. Perhaps go for a hike in your nearest park instead, or give parents a newsletter with information about your nearest state or national park and tips for what they could do with their toddlers there on their own time.

Remember that hiking up and down is going to be a lot more work for a little toddler's legs. Keep this in mind when determining the appropriate length of your hike. This is one of those times that the journey, not the destination, is the point.

**NOTICE** Follow your toddlers' lead. Stop when they want to look at something closer.

Pause for a snack or water break when they need it.

Pay attention to how far you've gone. Give a concrete warning before you turn around such as, "When we get to that tree, we are going to head back to the picnic area to play a game." Head back before they get too tired.

# Activities

## Laminated COLLECTION

On your walk, gather some leaves, flowers, etc. I find it helpful to pick one thing to look for to give your walk some focus. Then, make a laminated collection when you return.

### What to Do

**Materials**
Found objects
Heavy books or boxes
Laminator or contact paper
Basket
Magnifying glasses (optional)
Photos (optional)

1. When you get back, flatten some of your collection under a stack of books or something heavy.

2. Then, laminate your collection and place the items in a basket for your toddlers to explore. I encourage you to put some of your collection out for your toddlers to explore with all of their senses, but laminating your collection will increase the items' durability and potentially be friendlier for younger toddlers who like to mouth everything.

3. For older toddlers, I recommend adding some extra tools for exploration, such as magnifying glasses or pictures to compare their objects to, in order to increase their interest and learning.

## NATURE Walk TAPE Bracelets

Nature bracelets are easy to make and a perfect activity for hikes or camping.

**Materials**
Duct tape

### What to Do

1. Tape a piece of duct tape around each child's arm with the sticky side facing out.

2. Then as you walk, encourage them to collect small items to add to their bracelets.

3. When you are done with your walk, they will have fun nature-themed bracelets.

4. If they are interested, talk to them about the items on their bracelets. Show interest in the things that they found interesting on your walk.

# Start a NATURE Collection

Do your toddlers like to collect things wherever they go, such as flowers, rocks, and sticks? If they are filling your pockets and the diaper bag, it is time to start a nature collection.

## What to Do

1. Find a space that can be devoted to your children's nature collection. A tray and low table are ideal, but work with what you have.

2. Help them carefully place their items and materials such as a magnifying glass, notepad, and pencil nearby to help them investigate further.

## Materials
Tray or low table
Collected materials
Notepad and pencil
Magnifying glasses
Tweezers

Tip: The younger the toddler, the simpler this will need to be. For example, my twins had a pinecone collection when they were very tiny toddlers. Every time we went for a walk, they collected pinecones and then added them to a basket on one of their shelves. They often used the pinecones in their play. For older toddlers, as you notice a focus (rocks, for instance), provide them with photos and books on their interest to extend learning.

# Ocean or Lake

**M**ost children love water: the bathtub, water tables, and splashing in the sink, even throwing things in the toilet. If you have water lovers, plan a trip to the largest body of water in your area. Depending on what the body of water is and the season during which you are visiting, your activities there will vary.

Please practice water safety. Low adult-child ratios are especially important for such activities. I highly recommend no more than two to three children per adult. This is an adventure for either parents on their own time or for classes to engage a lot of extra parent volunteers or staff.

**BRING**   Pack towels, dry clothes, sun protection, buckets, and shovels.

**NOTICE**   Wade in the water, notice how it moves, splash the water, feel it run through your hands. Use a bucket and pour some water on sand or rocks nearby. Explore and encourage your children to explore.

## Activities

One of the things that fascinates toddlers the most about the beach is sand. The texture is unlike anything else, and for sensory curious little beings, the beach is filled with textural delights. Explore those textures with this easy and fun mystery bag.

## BEACH
### Mystery Bag

## What to Do

1. Place the items inside your bag without your children seeing them.

2. Invite your toddlers over to help you solve a mystery. Have them reach their hands in the bag and find one object.

3. Encourage them to explore it with their fingers inside the bag or with their eyes closed.

4. Ask them to describe what they feel.

5. Then have them pull it out and look at the object they have picked.

6. For older toddlers, invite them to reach back in and feel for a matching object. Continue exploring the items until they are all matched. Younger toddlers might be interested in matching pairs as they pull them out of the bag.

7. Place the materials on your shelf for further exploration.

## Materials

Cloth bag
Pairs of beach-themed items
for each child such as:
  2 seashells
  2 sandpaper squares
  2 pairs of goggles

# WATER
## Pictures

Paint with water, a classic summer activity. This is best to try on a hot summer day.

## What to Do

1. Fill a bucket with water and place it with paintbrushes near a smooth surface you can get wet. Flat, somewhat smooth surfaces are best. Fences, sides of buildings, and sidewalks all work well.

2. Model how to paint the wall with your paintbrush.

3. Remark on their painting, and talk about the different types of brush strokes they can use.

## Materials

Bucket of water (1 for
  every 2–4 toddlers)
Paintbrush (1 per child)

Tip: The toddlers I've worked with have always been a little dubious that I was actually okay with them "painting" the wall. They often needed me to model painting with water before they eagerly joined me.

# Inside BEACH PARTY

One of my favorite (and only) memories of my preschool experience was when we had a beach party inside our classroom. When I became a teacher, I knew this was something I wanted to attempt to duplicate. This is good, silly pretend play.

## What to Do

1. Lay out your beach towels and your chosen beach props ahead of time. If you are offering water play, you may want to do this outside.

2. Prep your toddlers like you would for other water play: strip them down to diapers or put them in their swimsuits or summer clothes, and talk to them about your beach party.

3. Allow your toddlers to take the lead investigating everything you have laid out. Describe what they are doing, and emphasize new words about the beach towel, water, bucket, etc.

4. Older children might enjoy helping you prep the activity or brainstorm a list of things you would need at a beach party.

## Materials

Big beach towels
Buckets
Toys for dumping in and filling buckets
Large container (the older the child, the larger the container)
Water or sand
Cups for scooping and dumping
Goggles and other fun beach accessories
Swimwear or summer clothes (optional)

## Scavenger Hunt: Beach

When visiting the beach, search for these items with toddlers for fun.

| | | |
|---|---|---|
| Seashell | Seagull | Bucket with sand |
| Beach umbrella | Cloud | Paddleboard |
| Boat | Sunscreen | Polka-dot swimsuit |
| Feet buried in sand | Safety notice | Kite |

# Night Walk

It can be difficult for toddlers when the evenings start to get dark. Their concept of time is thrown off, which often causes anxiety. There are, however, some positives, and one of them is the ability to take a night walk without waiting for it to be really late.

In our center, shortly after daylight savings time had ended, we often went for a short walk with flashlights outside with a small group. This was a fun distraction for the fact that afternoons seem confusing and long to children when it suddenly gets dark so early.

**BRING** Pack your flashlights and try to wear reflective clothing.

**CONSIDER** For younger toddlers especially, don't feel like you have to wait until it is pitch black. Just darker than when you would normally be outside will work great.

**NOTICE** Lay some ground rules, such as staying together and stepping carefully, and head outside to explore a familiar spot in the dark.

See what they notice. What can they spy with their lights? What do they hear? How do they feel about the dark?

## Activities

### Flashlight SHAPE Hunt

Inside is now dark too. Take advantage and put those toddlers to work with their flashlights inside.

## What to Do

1. Cut out shapes and tape them around your home, playroom, or classroom. For younger toddlers you might want to focus on one shape. For older children, cut a variety of shapes. For even older children, you can adapt this game by looking for letters, numbers, or even sight words.

### Materials

Construction paper
Tape
Scissors (adult use)
Flashlights (one per child)

2. Once the shapes are hidden around your play space (and the sun is starting to go down), invite your toddlers to do a flashlight hunt.

3. Explain what they are searching for and possibly show them an example.

4. Then, explain you will be doing this in the dark with your flashlights.

5. Help them turn their flash lights on, and then turn the overhead light off.

6. Let the hunt begin.

# WHITE on BLACK Illustrations

Offer an invitation to create with black construction paper and light-colored chalk.

## What to Do

1. Lay out a piece of black paper and several light-colored pieces of chalk for each child. This is an entirely open-ended activity. Your toddlers are exploring chalk, light and dark, and making marks on a paper.

2. The light colors contrast with the black, creating a visually exciting contrast. For some extra motivation, read a book such as *Night Animals* by Gianna Marino first, and briefly discuss the illustrations before they start drawing.

### Materials

Black construction paper
Chalk
*Night Animals* by Gianna Marino (optional)

# STAR STICKER Pictures

Stickers are a wonderful material for toddlers. There is the pleasant fact that they are pretty low mess and enjoyable, but more important, they are wonderful for developing a pincer grasp, a fine motor skill.

## What to Do

1. Place a page of star stickers and some black paper on a table for your toddlers.

2. When they wander over, invite them to make a starry night picture like the sky you (hopefully) saw on your walk.

Tip: Some toddlers have difficulty removing stickers from the page. Instead of doing it for them, scaffold their skill development by bending back the sticker page so the sticker is half off the backing. You can do this one row at a time, allowing them to be largely independent.

### Materials
Black construction
  paper
Star stickers

# Science
# Museum

Science museums are a great place to explore all kinds of topics, such as weather, our bodies, how things move, etc. For children with lots of questions, the science museum will provide both answers and a whole host of new things to wonder about.

When planning a trip to a science museum, check out the website before you go. See what exhibits they have, to give you an idea of what might interest your children.

**BRING** Pack water and snacks so you can take a break as their typical schedule dictates.

**CONSIDER** Plan to go during a time when your children are well rested and have full bellies. Make sure to leave before they get overtired or hungry, to avoid meltdowns. Early mornings are often great for happy children and less crowded museums.

**NOTICE** Follow your children's lead. Don't feel like you need to see everything every trip.

## Activities

This is kind of like I Spy for toddlers. There isn't any guessing involved, just an exercise in looking more closely at the world. You can do this at home or wherever you are. It is sometimes fun to play this on a walk.

Play THREE
Things I SEE

## What to Do

1. Invite your children to play "Three Things."

2. You can start by saying, "I see a red truck, a ball, and a striped shirt."

3. Your toddlers will likely try to spot these items. Start with at least two fairly obvious ones and maybe one that is a little hard to spot. Maybe that ball rolled under a table.

4. Then ask the children what three things they see.

## Materials
None

# SORT by BIG and SMALL

Sorting is an important math skill for toddlers to practice. They will be more inclined to work on this if you present objects they are interested in at the moment.

## Materials
Items of different sizes
Basket

## What to Do

1. Gather items for sorting. Some ideas include sorting pinecones or animals by size, sorting trains by color, or sorting dinosaurs by what they eat. The younger your toddlers, the simpler this needs to be.

2. You can do this during group time, as a small group, or just during play time. When and what toddlers are interested in varies. Some toddlers may want to sit and sort every item in your basket. Some toddlers will be only moderately interested in having you label which item is big and which is little. Either extreme or somewhere in the middle is okay.

3. Repeat this activity with different materials and at different times. I've even done this during snack. You could ask, "Who has a really BIG carrot?" or "Who sees a really small blueberry?"

# BEAN BAG
## Body TOSS

Toddlers love learning about themselves. This is a fun activity to practice the names of body parts and a little gross motor development.

## What to Do

1. Find some bean bags (rolled socks work in a pinch).

2. Trace each toddler's body on the ground with chalk or on a large piece of paper, to play inside.

3. Then, play a bean bag toss game in which you name a body part and they toss the bean bag to that part on the child's chalk outline. For example, "Where's your head?"

4. For older toddlers, use more difficult vocabulary such as *elbow, ankle* or *neck*, or phrase the question by what the body part does, for example, "What part do you use for walking?"

### Materials
Bean bags
Chalk or markers
and paper

# Tree Walk

**D**o you have a favorite tree? When we lived in Mississippi, it was the gorgeous magnolia tree hanging into our backyard. The flowers were stunning, and we loved creating with the large, thick leaves when they fell. Do your children notice trees? Do they look up at them or comment about their leaves changing? If so, take them for a tree walk.

This can happen down your street, on your playground, at a park, or in a larger forested area. Wherever you go, talk first about how you are going to look more closely at trees. Ask the children to tell you what they know about trees. Use those answers as a starting point when you are on your walk.

**BRING**     Pack binoculars or magnifying glasses and paper and crayons for rubbings. You may also want to pack a camera and bags for collecting.

**CONSIDER**     Expect that their interest might wander or last for only a little while. If you get five to ten minutes of engaged interest, you are doing great.

**NOTICE**     On your walk, notice different trees. Encourage your children to touch the bark; see if they can wrap their arms around the trunk; and look for leaves, acorns, or other tree offerings on the ground around the tree.

# Activities

## Compare Seasons: PHOTO and BOOK

This is perfect for a tree that changes with the seasons that you can easily see and visit repeatedly.

### What to Do

1. Help your toddlers take pictures of the whole tree.

2. Write down their observations. What color are the leaves? Has anything fallen off of the tree? Can they wrap their arms all the way around the tree?

3. If they are interested and capable, have them draw their own pictures of what the tree looks like.

4. Then make a note on your calendar to visit the tree three, six, and nine months from now.

5. When the time comes, repeat the same process as above.

6. For a shorter activity, try viewing a tree at the end of winter and then again a month later.

## BARK Rubbing

This is another simple example of rubbings, which is a great activity for fine motor development but also for exploring texture.

### What to Do

1. For bark rubbings, go outside to a tree and put the paper over the tree.

2. Hold it (or tape it) while your toddlers use crayons to rub the tree's impression onto the paper.

3. When they are done, invite them to compare the image with the real bark. What do they notice?

# LEAVES and ACORNS Sensory Bin

This is a perfect fall sensory bin.

## Materials

Sensory bin or table
Leaves and acorns
    or other loose
    natural materials
Bowls, scoops,
    measuring cups

## What to Do

1. Find a tub and gather plenty of leaves and acorns.

2. Provide little bowls or cups to hold the acorns.

3. Leave the tub in a space that can get a little messy, for your toddlers to explore. While they play they are exploring texture, number, capacity, and more.

Safety note: Supervise the children around small items, and consider the children's ages and abilities when choosing items.

# Spotlight on Loose Parts and Natural Materials

One of the many things about Reggio-inspired practices that inspires me is their use of real, natural materials throughout their environments. Infants and toddlers learn through hands-on explorations of their world. They have a natural curiosity about the things around them. Young infants watch sunlight stream through leaves, pull at the grass with their fingers, and wiggle their toes in the sand. Choosing beautiful, diverse, and natural materials demonstrates respect for this process and for the child. Furthermore, these materials support the child's development of knowledge and ability to attend. To me, the inclusion of natural materials and the importance of loose parts go together. Both naturally encourage creativity and curiosity. Both value the child and view him as a competent, creative, inquisitive person.

Since I have been home with my twins, I have mulled over how to fine-tune our environment and expand our explorations weekly. Introducing them to a wide array of creative experiences was instinctive, but I struggled more with incorporating natural materials and loose parts when they were infants. Their tendency to mouth everything in sight made me hesitate to bring natural materials into our home, yet I started little by little. I learned that with supervision and intriguing invitations, their explorations tended to be more engaged. (I also grew to accept that some mouthing would happen as they used all of their senses to investigate the materials.) Gradually, we have expanded the materials available in their environment. It is evident that these open-ended materials encourage children to be inventive and to experiment. The limitless possibilities of such materials draw them to tinker and create.

Here are some of the loose parts and natural materials that were offered to them in their first two years:

**INFANTS:**

Flowers | Grass | Large Rocks | Leaves | Pinecones | Sticks | Yarn

**TODDLERS:**

everything above, plus

Acorns | Beads | Can Lids | Nuts and Bolts | Pebbles | Seashells

Seeds | Tree Bark | Washers

**WE HAVE PRESENTED THESE MATERIALS ALONG THE**
**LOOSE PARTS AND NATURAL ITEMS:**

Building Blocks | Clay | Glass Jars | Glue | Paint | Playdough

Soil | Clear Containers | Water | Light

This is in no way an exhaustive list, but hopefully it is a good place to get started.

# Garden

Find a public garden and schedule time for a visit. If you are doing this in warmer months, there is likely to be an abundance of options. Even in winter months, many areas have indoor gardens you can visit. If you don't have a garden within walking distance, perhaps there is a park that makes some effort with their landscaping. This can also work for this adventure idea in a pinch.

**BRING** Plan to pack cameras or binoculars and something for your toddlers to do with their hands, to avoid spending the entire time reminding them not to pick every flower in sight.

Drawing journals and crayons are a good addition to your packing list.

**CONSIDER** Talk to your toddlers about what they will see and how to be gentle with the flowers. At home or school, practice touching gently with your own flowers or something else delicate such as leaves or even your hand before you go.

**NOTICE** Invite your toddlers to gently touch petals if that is allowed, to smell the flowers, and to show you their favorites. Talk to them about the parts of the flower to help expand their vocabulary.

# Activities

## Take PHOTOS of FLOWERS

Toddlers are more capable than you might think of taking photos with a little instruction, and their view of the world is interesting. After they've had some general practice taking pictures, as described on page 119, giving them a focus for their photos can be fun.

### What to Do

1. Encourage them to take pictures of flowers in a garden you visit, on a walk, or in your yard.

2. Ask them questions such as, "What colors do you see?" or "Do you see the stem through your camera?"

3. After they are satisfied with taking pictures, download the pictures onto the computer and print them out if possible. If you are doing this in a classroom, this step may not be possible. In that case, print off several photos, and then move on to the next stage of the activity.

4. Look at the pictures together and invite them to tell you about their favorites.

5. Consider making a book with the photos. Children love looking back over what they've done and sharing it with others.

### Materials

Cameras (1 per child)
Flowers

## PETAL Collage

This is another contact-paper collage idea. It would also work with glue if you prefer.

### What to Do

1. Gather some flowers and break off the petals. Your toddlers might enjoy helping you with this.

2. Place all the flower petals in a basket or bowl next to contact paper with the sticky side up.

3. Invite your toddlers to create a collage with the petals on the contact paper.

4. When they are done you can stick it to a window.

### Materials

Flowers
Contact paper

# TAPE
## Flower
## ART

Use a toddler favorite supply to make some flowers. You can likely think of your own spin on this activity, but to get you started I am going to give you the simplest idea.

## What to Do

1. Before the activity, tear or cut strips of tape for your toddlers to use. Attach them to a large block that the toddlers can then pull off to create their picture.

2. Tear strips of green paper to use as stems. With younger toddlers, I would skip the stem prompt entirely and let them make a colorful tape picture.

3. Show your toddlers how to glue the green stems to the white paper.

4. Then, invite them to add petals. Washi tape is easy to tear, so older toddlers can probably manage; otherwise, give them a pair of child-size scissors to use to cut pieces.

5. Older toddlers are also more likely to understand where petals should go on a flower, but regardless, enjoy the process and knowledge that your children are learning to use tools, developing fine motor skills, and expanding their creativity.

## Materials

White paper
Green paper
Washi or other colored tape
Glue stick
Large block
Child-safe scissors (optional)

# Climb a Mountain

Toddlers are among the smallest people in our world, and they often feel small. If you watch toddlers, they will often work hard to climb playground structures, chairs, tables, and whatever else they can find to feel bigger and taller. If there is a hill in your area, take a field trip to the top with your toddlers.

**BRING** You may need to pack water, snacks, sunscreen, and a camera.

**CONSIDER** What seems like a small hill to you can feel like a mountain to your toddlers. Tell them you are going to climb a tall mountain and see what you can see! Be patient as you climb, as walking on an incline will be challenging for some newer walkers. It is also a good gross motor development activity, so encourage them to walk us much as they can.

This would be challenging with children who have limited gross motor capabilities. For very young toddlers, it may be possible to use a backpack carrier if the parent has one available.

**NOTICE** Try making up songs to sing to encourage your toddlers and enjoy the climb. For example, "We are going up up up, up up up, up up up. We are going up up up. Up to the very top." Singing like this allows for creativity and may help develop your toddlers' language skills.

# Activities

This block activity is simple and can occur naturally in play.

## How High CAN YOU BUILD?

### What to Do

1. While your children stacks blocks, talk about how a tower is tall or short, or you can challenge your toddlers to see how high they can build.

2. Through trial and error during this play, your toddlers will discover how to build a well-supported tower.

3. You are also modeling comparative language such as *tall, taller,* and *tallest*.

**Materials**
Blocks

Sing the song "The Bear Went Over the Mountain" with your toddlers.

## Sing Songs: The BEAR Went over the MOUNTAIN

### What to Do

1. March your legs as you go up the mountain.

2. Actively search to "see what you can see."

3. Then, march back down.

**Materials**
None

(Sing to the tune of "For He's a Jolly Good Fellow.")

*The bear went over the mountain,*
*The bear went over the mountain,*
*The bear went over the mountain,*
*To see what he could see.*

*And all that he could see,*
*And all that he could see,*
*Was the other side of the mountain,*
*The other side of the mountain,*
*The other side of the mountain,*
*Was all that he could see.*

*The bear went over the river,*
*To see what he could see.*
*And all that he could see,*
*Was the other side of the river,*
*The other side of the river,*
*Was all that he could see.*

# Cardboard
# BINOCULARS

If you have child-size binoculars, that is awesome. The more times you can put real tools into toddlers' hands to use, the better. If not, you can make your own binoculars.

## What to Do

1. First, have each toddler decorate two paper-towel tubes.

2. Then, punch two holes at the top of each tube.

3. Thread the string or ribbon through and tie a knot, leaving a long loop that can go around a toddler's neck.

4. After you have used them inside a little bit, take the binoculars on your next adventure outside.

5. At home, we hung ours near our doorway on hooks for easy access before an adventure. In a classroom, I might collect them all in a basket and place it on a shelf near the door to outside.

6. They do not magnify anything, obviously, but they do seem to help children focus their attention on something such as birds or flowers when you go for a hike.

## Materials

Paper-towel tubes, cut in half
String or ribbon
Hole punch
Tape
Decorative tape or markers
Scissors (adult only)

# Farm

I do realize that I mentioned farms in the Animals section, but there are many reasons to visit a farm. One of our favorites is to harvest crops such as blueberries, apples, or pumpkins. The animals are fun, but drawing the connection between farms and the food that we eat is also a great reason to head to the country.

**BRING** Wear clothes that can get dirty. Dirt and food stains are highly probable.
Pack sunscreen and a change of clothes.
Wipes and a full diaper bag are a good idea.
You might bring a camera to take photos of your visit.

**CONSIDER** For classes, the farm should be within walking distance for the teacher to push children in a stroller. Otherwise, your options are to visit a grocery store or farmers' market, again with a focus on fruits or vegetables, or to send home a note to the parents about local farms they could visit and how best to engage their children in the experience.

# Activities

## IN and OUT Containers

If you are picking blueberries, strawberries, or apples, a large portion of what you will be doing is putting fruit into a container. The concept of in versus out is one that young toddlers are developing.

### What to Do

1. Offer your toddlers the chance to practice more at home or in the classroom by providing a variety of containers with some large pompoms to put in and take out.

**Materials**
Containers
Large pompoms
Spoons or large tweezers (optional)

2. If your toddlers are older, provide spoons or large tweezers to increase the difficulty.

## Sorting FOOD by COLOR

Sorting can work for so many different materials. This is a food-inspired sorting activity. This is a fun activity to do during snack time. Sort some food, eat some food, and have fun talking about colors and healthy food along the way.

### What to Do

1. Gather various foods, such as a selection of berries. You will need a piece of construction paper for each color represented. Different types of apples, a variety of fruit, and cans of food would also work well.

**Materials**
Food examples in various colors
Piece of construction paper for each color
Marker
Bowl

2. Wash all of the food, and place it in a bowl together.

3. Then invite your toddlers to help you sort by color. Spread out the construction-paper pieces, labeling each color for or with your toddlers (depending on their ages) as you place it in front of them.

4. Then pull out a berry, and ask them to find the color that matches.

5. Older children might enjoy sorting types of food, such as sorting fruits and vegetables.

# Veggie
# PRINTMAKING

Potatoes, carrots, and peppers are all great for print-making.

## What to Do

1. Depending on what you are learning, what you picked at the farm, and what you have available, pick a fruit or vegetable that works best for you.

2. Pour some paint on paper plates.

3. Cut the vegetable in half. Place it alongside a plate with paint and a piece of paper.

4. Invite your toddlers to make prints by dipping the vegetables in the paint and then stamping them several times on the paper.

## Materials

Vegetables such as potatoes, carrots, or peppers
Knife (for adult use)
Paper
Paint

# Listening Walk

Developing the senses is a crucial part of toddler education. A lot of time is spent on developing and engaging the senses of sight and touch, but the other senses are often somewhat neglected. Our sense of hearing is particularly important and overlooked. Hearing is important for language development skills, among other things, and this activity helps to develop the ability to listen.

**CONSIDER**

Tell your toddlers that you are going for a walk, and you are going to listen to the sounds around you. Ask them to tell you some things that you might hear.

If you want to, write these ideas down.

Then explain that you are going to walk for a bit, and then you are going to take some listening breaks.

**NOTICE**

Walk a little way until you think you are in a good area for listening and invite your toddlers to take a listening break with you.

Have them close their eyes and cover them with their hands and "open their ears."

Covering their eyes with their hands is helpful in reminding them to keep their eyes closed.

Let them listen for a moment and then ask what they heard.

Repeat this process a few times, making note of what they hear.

## Creating SOUND Patterns

This is a fun movement activity that also works on making simple patterns.

**Materials**
None

### What to Do

1. Make a simple ABA pattern using your body. Try something like clap, stomp, clap. Do it first, and then ask your toddlers to imitate you.

2. Older toddlers might be able to alternate. They clap, you stomp, they clap.

3. Some other ideas include singing a note, smacking your lips, or making animal noises. You can also create sound patterns using musical instruments.

4. With younger toddlers who aren't quite ready to work on making patterns, just have fun moving your bodies. Move your body and ask them to imitate what you did. For example, "I can stomp, stomp. Can you do it?"

5. If they do something fun with their bodies, feel free to label what you observe them doing and then imitate it back to them.

## DIY SOUND Matching Boxes

Sound matching boxes are a fun material often found in Montessori classrooms. They can be expensive to purchase, but luckily you can make your own.

**Materials**
Even number of small boxes or opaque jars with lids
Sets of 2 Items that make noise (bells, rice, etc.)

### What to Do

1. Gather an even number of small boxes or opaque jars with lids. You can also make some using cardboard and tape.

2. Fill sets of boxes with different items that will make noise when you shake them. For example, two with bells, two with a block, two with rice, two with marbles, two with a plastic block. Put the lids on.

3. Lay the boxes out and invite your children to help you match by shaking and listening for the same sound.

4. Your toddlers will likely want to peek inside right away, but encourage them not to spoil the secret.

5. Have them put the boxes near their ears and listen to the sound. Explain that every sound has a secret match. Can they find it?

# Play
# MUSICAL
## Instruments

Musical instruments are a great material to have in your home or classroom.

**Materials**
Variety of instruments,
1 per child

## What to Do

We have a basket with instruments available that I pull out occasionally for group activities or specific games. There are a lot of uses for musical instruments, but here are some basic ones to get you started: play instruments while you sing a favorite song or while you listen to different types of music. Practice opposites with music—for example, play soft/loud, high/low, fast/slow. Become a marching band and march while playing your instruments around the house or classroom.

# Conclusion

Learning opportunities are endless. That's the beauty of childhood, education, and, ultimately, life. We are the ones who create the limitations. Too often we fail to notice what interests children or to encourage them when we do.

We are constrained by the structure of seasons or themes that we return to religiously year after year. We believe that because it is a certain season or because the children are a certain age that they should be learning about a particular thing and then move on at another predetermined time.

The best learning is internally motivated and joyful. It is formed through a spark of interest, an observed event, an amazing book or character, a question. Once the interest is sparked, we are driven to find out more, to learn. When we take advantage of that, we can support deep and meaningful learning, even in the youngest of children. When we ignore it or limit it, we do a disservice to our children.

The ideas in this book are meant to be a starting point. They are meant to spark ideas and encourage you to look at the possibilities for learning in the world around you.

No child will be interested in all the explorations I have laid out. Some children will latch on to one or two ideas and will follow that all year if you let them. Some children will flit from thing to thing with interests as vast as our diverse world. Some explorations or activities will not work for your situation, setting, or the abilities of the children in your group.

Use this book as a place to begin. From there, the possibilities are endless.

# Glossary of Terms

**Cognitive Development**—the construction of thinking processes such as problem solving and remembering. In teaching, this area often also includes the learning of basic concepts and information.

**DIY**—stands for Do It Yourself. Often used to describe crafting your own version of something that someone would typically purchase

**Fine Motor Development**—building skill and strength in small muscles, primarily in the hands and fingers. This development is crucial for a variety of self-help skills as well as for writing.

**Gross Motor Development**—building skill, strength, coordination, and endurance of large muscles in arms and legs

**Imitation**—one of the earlier learning strategies employed by children where they mimic the people and behaviors they observe

**Invitation**—in education, this is often used to describe thoughtfully placing materials to prompt creativity or play for children to discover. This is frequently used with the term *strewing*; see below.

**Language Development**—this includes learning to talk but also vocabulary development, listening skills, and often other literacy skills.

**Montessori**—a method of teaching developed by Dr. Maria Montessori that focuses on child-directed learning based on scientific observations of development

**Older Toddlers**—for the purposes of this book, older toddlers are defined as twenty-four to thirty-six months of age. What children can do at a given age will vary greatly, but this is intended to give a general idea of when skills and activities can be appropriate.

**One-to-One Correspondence**—the understanding that, when counting, you apply one number to one object

**Parallel Play**—this is the second stage in the development of play skills. Instead of playing on their own (solitary play), older infants or young toddlers begin playing side by side with another child. Their play is not yet cooperative, but there is some interaction and imitation.

**Preliteracy**—skills that lay the foundation for reading, writing, and communicating

**Printmaking**—a category of art where images or pictures are made by using an object to make a print on paper with paint or ink

**Reggio Emilia**—an educational philosophy developed after World War Two by Loris Malaguzzi and families in villages around Reggio Emilia, Italy, that focuses on viewing children as capable and active contributors to their education and society. Programs that attempt to follow this philosophy are often called *Reggio inspired*.

**Scaffolding**—teaching practice of helping children learn a new skill by assisting just enough to help them achieve one step more complicated than they are able to do independently

**Self-Help Skills**—development of abilities to carry out basic self-care and daily routines independently. These include things such as zipping a coat, brushing teeth, using the bathroom, etc.

**Sensory Table or Sensory Bin**—a common addition to early childhood classrooms, this is a table or container that holds sensory materials such as sand, water, or rice. Sometimes called a *water table*

**Social/Emotional Development**—a broad area that encompasses building skills in a variety of areas, including interactions with others, relationships with caregivers, emotional regulation, self-expression, sense of self, and more

**STEM**—an increasingly popular movement to increase science, technology, engineering, and math opportunities in learning

**Strew or Strewing**—a term coined by blogger Sandra Dodd. This is the art of allowing your child to discover something you have casually left for her to find

**Younger Toddler**—for the purpose of this book, younger toddlers are defined as twelve to twenty-four months of age. This is merely to give you general guidelines for what might be appropriate. Individual children will vary greatly in the natural course of development.

# References

Buhr, Erin. 2015. Bambini Travel. "30+ Ways of Learning Through Adventure." Last Modified October 30, 2015, http://www.bambinitravel.com/Pages/BTBlog/blogitem.php?id=120

Druckerman, Pamela. 2012. *Bringing up BéBé: One American Mother Discovers the Wisdom of French Parenting*. London: Penguin Press.

Galinsky, Ellen. 2010. *Mind in the Making: The Seven Essential Life Skills Every Child Needs*. New York: Harper Studio.

Gettman, David. 1988. *Basic Montessori: Learning Activities for Under-Fives*. New York: St. Martin's Griffin.

Hughes, Holly. 2009. *Frommer's 500 Places to Take Your Kids Before They Grow Up*. 2nd ed. New York: Frommers.

Lewin-Benham, Ann. 2010. *Infants and Toddlers at Work: Using Reggio-Inspired Materials to Support Brain Development*. 2nd ed. New York: Teachers College Press.

Lillard, Paula Polk, and Lynn Lillard Jessen. 2003. *Montessori from the Start: The Child at Home, from Birth to Age Three*. New York: Schocken.

Wurm, Julianne P. 2005. *Working in the Reggio Way: A Beginner's Guide for American Teachers*. St. Paul, MN: Redleaf Press.

# Index